The Continuing Heritage

Lionel Esher

FRANEY

Front cover
Brasenose College, Oxford (A 1963 — see page 83)

Back cover
Biddick Farm Arts Centre, Washington, Tyne and Wear (A 1979)

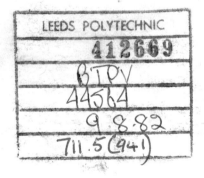
Published by
Franey & Co Ltd
2 Burgon Street, London EC4V 5DP

ISBN 0 900382 42 2

Filmset and Printed by
Chandlers (Printers) Ltd
Bexhill-on-Sea, East Sussex

Contents

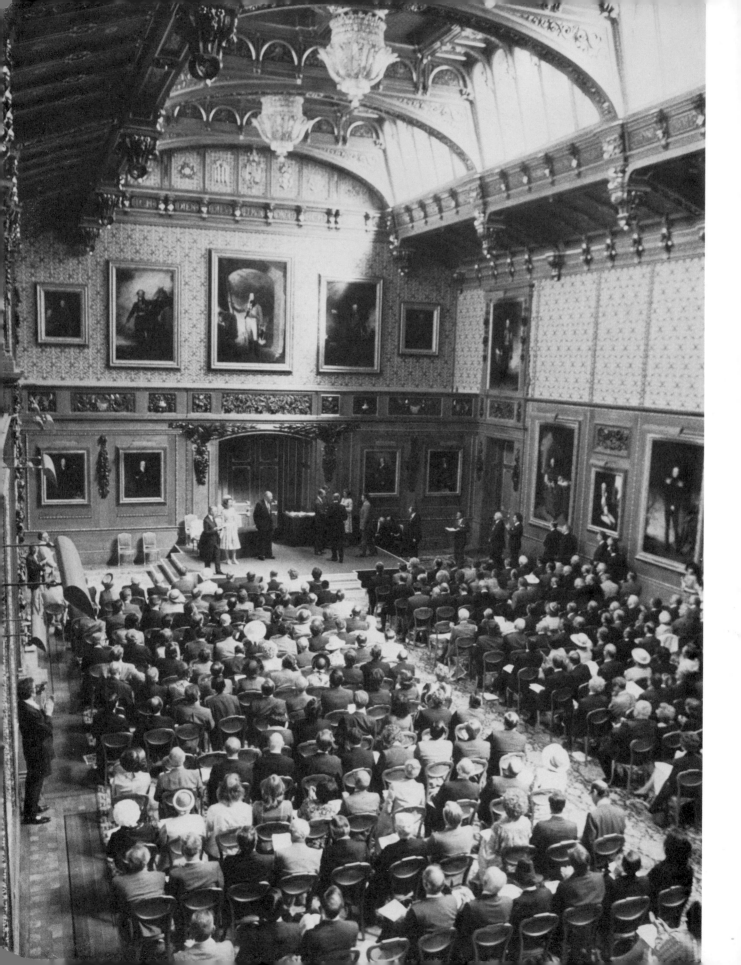

Foreword

by HRH The Duke of Edinburgh, KG, KT

Recent years have seen such an emphasis on the preservation of our heritage that it is rather refreshing to be reminded that we are also creating a heritage for future generations.

If there is anything to be learnt from past experience, it is that the best planning and architecture is usually sterile unless the planners and architects, as well as those who commission them, have a personal relationship with, and a civic pride in the community for whom they are working. Cities can only be created by their own citizens, otherwise they just become conurbations.

The significance of this book is that it has appeared at a time when Britain is more crowded than it has ever been before in history and consequently more and more of this country is being used for human habitation, industry and leisure. What is built in the next few years and how it is built is going to have a dramatic influence on the life of future generations.

The Heritage Year Awards presentation ceremony, in the Waterloo Chamber, Windsor Castle – June 1975

Author's note

This book results from the initiative of Michael Middleton, Director of the Civic Trust, who has kindly contributed its second chapter. I am also most grateful to Victor Rose of the Trust for the research which made it possible, and Barbara Manwill for compiling the Index

L.E.

Civic Trust

Founded in 1957, the Trust is a recognised charity supported by voluntary contributions. It encourages the protection and improvement of the environment. By means of conferences, practical projects, films and reports it focuses attention on major issues in planning and architecture. It publishes a bi-monthly journal *Heritage Outlook* and maintains a library and photographic collection. It makes Awards for good development of all kinds. Among some particular concerns have been the initiation of co-operative street improvement schemes; the promotion of new techniques for transplanting semi-mature trees; industrial dereliction and urban wasteland; the problems of damage and disruption caused by heavy lorries. The Trust encourages the formation of local amenity societies and gives advice and support to over 1,000 such societies now on its register. Its proposals led to the creation of the Lee Valley Regional Park Authority. It was closely associated with the drafting of the Civic Amenities Act 1967, which created the concept of the Conservation Area, and the Town and Country Amenities Act 1974. At the request of the Government, it provided the United Kingdom Secretariat for European Architectural Heritage Year 1975. It administers the Architectural Heritage Fund, an independent charity which provides loan capital to local buildings preservation trusts; and on behalf of the Department of the Environment, the work of the Heritage Education Group. From 1973 to 1981 it has administered government grant-aid to conservation projects in non-outstanding conservation areas on behalf of the Historic Buildings Council. Associate Trusts are linked with it in the North West, the North East, Scotland and Wales.

Opposite page
Kingsgate Footbridge, Durham
(page 116)

CIVIC TRUST 17 CARLTON HOUSE TERRACE LONDON SW1Y 5AW (01-930 0914)

CHAPTER ONE

Changes of Climate

People's Architecture 1950-1956

'It was the best of times; it was the worst of times.' The worst thing about the Fifties was the time it took to move out of the shadow of war. The decade began with '1984,' with the sense of doom of a generation condemned to the eternal defence of obscure frontiers against another dingy régime. For Cyril Connolly, 'It is closing time in the gardens of the west,' and for Brecht

> He who laughs
> Has not heard the bad news.

The best things in life were no doubt free, but unobtainable.

But in this equality of non-opportunity social guilt and social envy were for a time dissolved. The best thing about the Fifties was that we were still, for those few years, One Nation. The Welfare State, the National Health Service, The Butler Education Act, the 1947 Planning Acts, the New Towns, the Abercrombie blueprints for London, were incontrovertibly good things, and to have a part in their implementation was to have a calling, not a mere job. To get the cost of a house below £1000, to devise modular systems that made elegant use of wartime technology, to turn out prefabs on aircraft assembly lines, all for unfailingly delighted beneficiaries, what could be more gratifying? In 1955 Margaret Willis, the LCC's sociologist, polling the tenants of the first eleven-storey 'point blocks' at Wimbledon, found that the higher off the ground they lived, the happier they were. Liverpool council tenants aspired to a new flat, not to be 'fobbed off' (as they put it) with a reconditioned terrace house. In the 'twilight areas' of all the inner cities, mouldy and peeling after a decade of neglect, the demand was for a clean slate and a new world.

The 1951 Festival of Britain set the tone, already familiar to readers of the *Architectural Review* from the tantalising sketches of Hugh Casson and Gordon Cullen. We would exploit the idiosyncrasies of old towns, consult the genius of the place, exploit visual accidents, subtle changes of direction and level, surprise glimpses, 'netted' views, barriers, naïve graphics, primary colours — as though 'we' owned the place. People were still content to be bespoken by the liberal intelligentsia. And the architectural equivalent of the New Look certainly went down well, in a society still hungry for the feminine arts, for domestic pleasures, and for artefacts contrived merely for fun. The two great monuments

Ulster Terrace, Regents Park, London (page 48)

of the Fifties, Coventry Cathedral and the Mark 1 Festival Hall, and the two most characteristic environments, the LCC's Lansbury estate in East London and the earlier neighbourhoods at Harlow, have been pretty popular ever since. 1951 was also the year in which Sir Robert Matthew persuaded the London County Council to abandon their stodgily designed walk-up flats and to accept the 'mixed development' of point-blocks, four-storey maisonettes and terrace houses under the Scandinavian influence which was already the hallmark of the New Towns, and to use it for the first stage of the romantically sited Roehampton project. Two years later Lewis Womersley's appointment to Sheffield carried the same housing policies across the Trent. Only a handful of local authorities, and only a thimbleful of private builders, produced two-storey housing of equally unaffected and apparently effortless design. In high density housing the outstanding project of the Fifties was Churchill Gardens in Westminster, won in competition as early as 1946 and built at the hitherto unprecedentedly high density of 200 persons per acre, to the applause of all concerned. The architectural consensus looked as effortless and secure as the political one.

The second breakthrough of the post-war decade was in the field of education. The shortage of teaching space was as critical as the shortage of houses. The Government from force of wartime habit could think of nothing better than 'hutments,' but some young architects in the Ministry of Education led by Stirrat Johnson-Marshall had the wit to transform this brief into terms of modular prefabrication of components, exploiting wartime arms factories and time-saving techniques, and a single county architect in Hertfordshire (C.H. Aslin) and his Director of Education (John Newsom) had the courage to give the system the size of programme it needed to achieve economies of scale. The result was a series of airy and freely assembled structures, expressive of liberal teaching ideas in the primary schools, which became a model to Britain and to Europe, not only for their economy but for their elegance.

These structures did more than solve an urgent social problem. They were symbolic of a bloodless architectural revolution which all concerned were convinced was irreversible. The battles of the Thirties against the Georgians, the Art-Decorators and the other stylists belonged to a vanished age, expunged by the war. A rational architecture, emerging unselfconsciously out of dedicated attention to human needs and resources, had asserted itself as the natural expression of a generation which had set itself the task of liberating the subject classes, the subject sex and the subject peoples of a world for which it still felt its traditional moral responsibility.

The public attitude to the architectural heritage was equally uncontentious. Obviously listed buildings must be kept, but the lists were as yet small, and there were so many bombed sites and so much dereliction that there was little threat to them from building programmes which were under licence until 1954 and consisted almost entirely of housing, schools and industrial buildings on virgin sites. When Ian Nairn produced his *Outrage* issue of the *Architectural Review* in 1955 it was the ham-fisted operations of borough engineers and the nasty designs of spec builders (given their head by Macmillan in 1953) which preoccupied him — concrete lamp-posts, 'prairie planning,' municipal gardening, wirescape, hoardings, conifer plantations, Things in Fields — and for which he coined the useful umbrella word SUBTOPIA. It was the profligate use of our scarcest resource, land, which was at issue. Urban developers and their architects were not yet seen as the menace they were soon to be regarded. At this stage it was not the scale of their operations so much as the low standard of the architects they liked to employ which irritated the *Review.* Soon after the war J.M. Richards had castigated the lumpish and illiterate office blocks that Government departments were content to lease from low-grade developers in inner London. Later the attack was switched to the universities, both Oxbridge and Redbrick, which should have known better.

Boom and Brutalism 1956-1968

Irony has for centuries been a component of the British survival kit, but it easily degenerates into cynicism. If the last phase of wartime unity was symbolised by the Coronation in 1953, many people would date the slide into cynicism from the Suez plot of 1956. That affront to liberal values gave Harold Macmillan's subsequent recovery a sour taste and led before long to the 'I'm all right, Jack' which became the theme of the boom years around 1960. These were the years in which we all learned to look after ourselves, the small fry by restrictive practices and cash transactions, the big fish by 'printing money' in commercial television or speculative office development.

They were also the years of the boom in babies. Projecting the 1961 Census gave a horrific 20 million population increase by the turn of the century, with motor vehicles, of which there were 5 million in 1950, exploding to 25 million by the time they reached an estimated saturation point in 2010. The London population would double, and would need to be dispersed in New Cities all over the south-east. In his *London 2000,* published in 1963, Prof. Peter Hall gave an expansive vision of the city-region of the future, laced with motorways and living the mobile life of the American west coast. In the same years the Buchanan team's *Traffic in Towns* dramatically demonstrated the urban implications, with multiple urban motorways integrated into the city's fabric by means of 'traffic architecture,' and pedestrians moving on a deck above the traffic from one 'environmental area' to another. In 1963 also Wilfred Burns published his Newcastle plan, which gave physical expression to Dan Smith's Tyneside Rennaissance, while Graeme Shankland did the same for the centre of Liver-pool. It was forecast that the great port would expand rapidly, and that 'in the national context of steady economic growth from year to year new industries are expected to flock to Merseyside'.

Such being the climate of opinion and the predictions of experts, architec-ture, in its traditional role as the mirror of society, now proceeded to reflect this tough, euphoric, acquisitive decade. A younger generation, of which Peter & Alison Smithson were the recognised intellectual leaders, had no patience with the bland, bricky and generally quite boring style that had become the hallmark of the Welfare State. 'Our generation must try and produce evidence that men are at work.' Their aggressively unlovable school at Hunstanton, won in com-petition in 1949 and opened to children in 1954, the same year as Le Cor-busier's seminal *Unité d'habitation* at Marseilles, was the first building to be labelled 'brutalist'. But the most spectacular victory of the masculine principle was won in London, on the drawing boards of the LCC, then the busiest hive of young architectural talent in Europe. The second instalment of the great

Roehampton estate included a parade of the great Corbusian concrete slabs which were soon to march across south and east London, some on their sides, some stood on their ends. In their South Bank showpiece the *jeunes féroces* of the LCC gave a parallel demonstration of the change of fashion from the elegant Festival Hall to the grim concrete bunkers and the ponderously balustraded walkways of the Arts Centre. Meanwhile in the private sector brilliant architects like Lasdun, Stirling and Gowan showed the Jekyll & Hyde character of modernism. Lasdun's Royal College of Physicians and his St. James's flats in London were exemplars of how uncompromisingly modern buildings could take their place in distinguished company, yet at Liverpool and Cambridge he showed how brutal they could also be. Similarly, Stirling & Gowan's Engineering building at Leicester University was an expressionist masterpiece, but Stirling's angry red buildings at Oxford and Cambridge were soon to cock a snook at gentlemanly values. What they were demonstrating (and good architects are generally demonstrating something) was that buildings which are 'frankly of their own time' can do more for the vitality of cities than modest efforts to 'fit in'. They were doing no more than the fashionable Victorians had done without hesitation and without criticism.

But more than anything it was the scale rather than the detail of the emergent townscape that scared the life out of people. This was partly (but only partly) dictated by financial and social imperatives. Central city uses that had hitherto fitted inconspicuously into odd corners, like hotels, car parks and telephone exchanges, suddenly exploded in size. Others, like universities, grew so large that they had to move out of town altogether, to everybody's loss. Leapfrogging land values forced office buildings, which had hitherto lined up along street frontages in the Parisian manner, to take a pace back and leap into the air like New Yorkers or Chicagoans. 'Forced,' of course, does them more than justice. In most cases the force came from them. An early example was the Shell complex on London's South Bank, which stretched the LCC's civilised model with depressing results and compounded the felony by insisting on a stodgy and inelegant design for its tower — a poor example to the army of towers that was to follow. Unwise regulations deliberately kept in being by the Douglas-Home Government imposed an impossible penalty on local authorities who wished to resist: it would have cost £7.5 million to refuse the 7:1 plot ratio of what is now New Scotland Yard. Provincial cities knuckled under without a fight, indeed often willingly surrendered to 'partnership' deals sold to them by glossy presentation. Simultaneously their housing committees, taken on continental sales tours by their architects, ordered prefabricated tower blocks by the dozen, encouraged by Labour and Tory competition to reach half a million starts a year. The desperate housing need and the cost of urban land could not be denied.

But neither could it be denied that the tall building was a key ingredient in the modernist prescription. 'Towers,' their verticality exaggerated in perspectives like the heights of British mountains in 19th century watercolours, had fine romantic associations as well as futurist/technocratic credentials. In 1956 even the sensitive and scholarly Lord Holford proposed a 250 ft tower to give 'scale and interest' to his piazza adjacent to St. Paul's, and it was no doubt the shock of discovering and then combating this which sent Lord Duncan-Sandys down the track which was to lead to the inauguration of the Civic Trust a year later and to the Civic Amenities Act of 1967. But 'towers' is just what most of them were not. Pusillanimity and/or parsimony cut them down to mere stumps, and in the

London of the Sixties only the curvaceous Millbank Tower, the bitterly-contested Knightsbridge Barracks and Centre Point, and the universally popular Post Office spindle deserved the description. Shaken by the visual damage many of them were doing, several city planning authorities rushed out High Buildings Policies which would encourage them here and forbid them there, but these were largely ineffective: it was hard enough in the prevailing climate to stop a high building and impossible to promote one in the right place.

Commercial developers, of course, had always done a lot of damage. In the 19th century they had torn the heart out of Georgian cities like London and Liverpool, while the railways cut the suburbs to ribbons. And in the 20th, between the wars, they had shoved their backsides up against Wren steeples and ruined Georgian squares. They had always turned out twice as big as their elderly neighbours, as though designed for a taller species. But with the leap into the air they could spoil a whole city, not just a street or a square. Small cities like Aberdeen and Halifax lost their Gothic silhouettes, perhaps for ever. On the other hand they could dramatize and enhance the skylines of large ones like Birmingham and Sheffield. As in the past, the balance sheet was a complex one. But few people could take this grand synoptic view. To most, their own village, urban or rural, had been assaulted and often the effects were devastating.

It was no consolation to those affected that British architecture of the Sixties was so highly-regarded internationally. Indeed as it became more sophisticated, the locals liked it less. If the characteristic buildings of the Fifties were the new schools, glassy, flat-roofed, stripped-down, spreading themselves generously in the elmy fields, their classrooms soaked in sunlight, the characteristic achievements of the Sixties were the new universities, or the clever new insertions into the old ones. Where the schools had been anonymous, the work of dedicated local authority teams, university architecture was highly personal, with the stamp of the 'prima donna' (as he was unkindly labelled). Where Fifties architecture had been rationalist and on the whole cheap, Sixties architecture was formalist and on the whole expensive. Its characteristic monuments, Spence's Sussex, Lasdun's East Anglia, Sheppard's Imperial College hostels, were Corbusian in inspiration, though often personalised or romanticized, like New Hall in Cambridge, St. Anne's in Oxford, or Powell & Moya's subtle Portland Stone inserts into both. Corbusian influence was equally dominant in housing, from the comparatively modest Foundling Estate in Bloomsbury by Patrick Hodgkinson to the Sheffield City Architect's vast and dramatic Park Hill. Occasional exceptions reversed the trend: Pimlico School was more eccentric and absurd than any university, York University more modest and economical than most big schools. All in all, they were great days for architects.

The Resistance 1968–1973

In 1968 occurred two events which became immediately symbolic and signalled the end of the post-war consensus. In Paris the students practically destroyed the paternalist, old-fashioned and complacently 'square' de Gaulle regime and permanently ruined his prestige. In London an off-the-peg block of tower flats called Ronan Point was wrecked by a gas explosion, and though the disaster was not tragic (nobody died) it was enough to trigger a national resolve that there be no more of such buildings. (In fact they were no longer on the drawing-boards, but there were plenty still in the pipeline and, by 1975, 384 of them had been built in London alone.) Like most historic turning-points these two events were culminations, not beginnings. The first student sit-in at Berkeley, California, had been in 1964 and the first ideological assault on the conventional wisdom of post-war planning and housing had been Jane Jacobs' brilliant *Death and Life of Great American Cities* in 1961. In fact all through the years of the resistance, the inspiration came from America, a country whose traditional idealism is vulnerable to bitter disappointment and where the consequent cynicism is less readily shrugged off than in Europe. Hard rock, Black Power, Marcusian New Left politics, the drug culture and the trauma of Vietnam were a potent brew, soon exported to Europe where it rapidly swamped the gentle protests of the Beatle generation and the Flower People. Increasingly as the Sixties wore on the counter-attack against what was happening in our cities and landscape became politicised and professional.

A much-publicized example of the new mood of conservationist militancy was Covent Garden in London, where 1968 saw the publication of the GLC report which proposed what looked at the time like a sensible mixture of new commercial development and the retention of the best of the old buildings. But by now, under the influence of Jane Jacobs, it was contended that what was at stake was not a few listed buildings but a community, however slummy and clapped-out its buildings might be. The fact that in a market economy no low-rent commercial premises occupying valuable sites can be protected from a high-rent incursion, whether into old buildings or new ones, was forgotten or concealed in order that the struggle could be presented as a class war. But the architectural implications were no less significant. From now on there was a popular presumption against what used optimistically to be called urban renewal, irrespective of its architectural merits.

These were new allies for the respectable architectural preservation societies whose father figure had been William Morris. Just as it was the threat to Carlton House Terrace and the loss of the old Adelphi and Waterloo Bridge that gave birth to the Georgian Group in the Thirties, so it was the destruction of the Euston 'Arch' and of the Coal Exchange near Billingsgate in 1962 that gave birth to the Victorian Society. But from now on concern was no longer confined to great monuments like these, but to the ordinary humanized environments to which anonymous generations had contributed. 'Piecemeal' renewal, a dirty word amid the urgencies of the Fifties, was to be the panacea of the Seventies. It was enshrined in two vital pieces of legislation; first the Civic Amenities Act of 1967 which created the Conservation Areas, of which there were to be some 5,750 by 1981: here the existing character was to be paramount, new buildings had to conform with it and here demolition of listed buildings was later to be brought under planning control; and second, in 1969, a new Housing Act which set up General Improvement Areas in which Government grants were for the first time made available to support wholesale rehabilitation rather than wholesale replacement. Two other documents of 1969 were part of the same movement of opinion. The Skeffington Report proposed the compulsory adoption of Public Participation, two words which were soon to be emasculated by facile absorption into the conventional procedures of planning. And in the weekly *New Society* a proposal was made for officially-designated free-for-all areas of 'Non-Plan,' an idea drawn on a dozen years later for the Thatcher

Government's 'Enterprise Zones.' By 1971, when the Roskill Commission's systematically evaluated proposal for a third London Airport at Cublington was officially jettisoned in deference to Sir Colin Buckanan's purely intuitive objections, the high planning of the Sixties was already in retreat, and a year later, with the rejection of the last of the Whitehall rebuilding plans (for Richmond Terrace) city centre renewal on the grand scale was in retreat too. Reinvigorated conservation societies played leading parts in both dramas.

While the forces of resistance organized themselved in these years, the flood of new building, unprecedented in English history, continued unabated; and while much of it was inevitably skimped and ill-considered, some of it was of high quality. In all the appropriate parts of England, brick made a come-back, generally funereally dark in tone. This was particularly noticeable in London where, under the influence of Darbourne & Darke's pioneering project along Vauxhall Bridge Road (designed as early as 1961), high-density low-rise court-yard housing rapidly took over from the tower flats, particularly in the work of the new architects' departments of the enlarged Boroughs, set up in 1965. An incidental advantage of these rough, bricky buildings was that they were less easily vandalized : a man in corduroy makes a less spectacular victim than a man in white tie and tails. For vandalism and the wild art of the graffitist, another symptom of the end of the social truce, played havoc with the pristine white precast concrete slabs, and with the various flimsy sheet materials which, in the days when speed and economy were vital, had seemed so elegant a component of 'light and dry' construction; and before long these materials revealed other expensive defects — poor insulation, poor adhesion and, worst of all, poor fire resistance. The collapse of Ronan Point was, in other words, a technical as well as a social landmark in post-war architectural history. All over the place, as the Seventies advanced, modern construction came unstuck and its failures contributed to the growing nostalgia for a world of thick walls, soft plaster and tiled or slated roofs that did not leak. Before long there were to be compellingly practical, as well as sentimental, reasons to think in these terms.

The Breakout 1973-1982

In 1973 occurred two events which transformed the positivism of the previous decade into a mood that varied between relief and despair. The first was the energy crisis induced by OPEC's quadrupling of the price of oil. The second was the publication of the 1971 Census, which cut back the population projections drastically to the modest figures current in the Fifties. All the assumptions of architects and planners had to be scrapped overnight. What were now needed were not system-built, light-weight, high-energy, mass-produced buildings, but what the RIBA President Alex Gordon called the 'Three L's' : Long Life, Loose Fit, Low Energy. Thick walls, small windows, highly-insulated attics became not merely fashionable in the reaction against modernism but sensible as well. At the same time highway planners, airport planners, public utility planners had to lower their sights drastically. The morale of both professions was scarcely improved by two other major upheavals of the mid-seventies. The first was the 'reform' of local government whereby the county boroughs, on the whole the most efficient units in the old system, lost their independence and

17

either became mere districts in enlarged counties run from elsewhere, or had superimposed on them 'metropolitan counties' which they considered entirely superfluous. Meanwhile the architects had to endure a campaign of vilification in the media which was unique in the world. This was in part a justified reaction against the gigantism which had seemed the only way to solve the public housing problem and the surest way to make a fortune in the private sector. But, bearing in mind the comparative modesty of the British scale in both fields, the violence of the attack must have had other causes, not least the nostalgia induced by the sense of national failure, of decline from greatness, that pervaded the Seventies.

The result was that the conservationist counter-revolution, which had seemed a necessary and civilised response to the pressures of the boom years, found itself in ad hoc alliance with the New Left. Right-wing journalists were briefed by Trotskyist drop-outs from the GLC Architects' Department, architectural historians descended from their ivory towers to join in, while country gentry stalwarts of the CPRE found embarrassing allies in the polytechnics, whose Anti-Motorway militants changed frighteningly at weekends into Hunt Saboteurs. The time-honoured view that new buildings are always an improvement on old ones, which was a half-truth, now gave place to the view that they are always a disimprovement, which was another. Architects, natural residents of the liberal Centre, were under savage fire from the two strongly-reinforced wings. The economic weather, ending in the housing cutbacks and the worst slump in the building industry since the early Thirties, was scarcely calculated to raise the spirits.

But they seemed to thrive on adversity. As the gloomy Seventies wore on the quality of new architecture rose as its quantity fell, proving once again that to good designers time matters more than money. In stylistic terms it was inevitably a period of transition. The fading fashion for Corbusian concrete still produced masterly buildings like Casson and Conder's Elephant House and Lasdun's National Theatre, while Miesian steel and glass in the hands of younger architects like Foster, Rogers, Farrell and Grimshaw produced buildings of extreme elegance. But alongside these classic fulfilments of the high hopes of modernism the romantic reaction proliferated in all sorts of directions. At its worst it produced, sometimes under pressure from well-meaning planners, Design Guides, absurd 'vernacular' shopping centres, or under market pressures masses of illiterate neo-Georgian. At a slightly higher level, commercial architects, mounting the red brick bandwagon, junked their glass or slate or plastic spandrels and churned out bright red and bronze glass facades of equal vulgarity. But good architects could now resort to period pastiche in suitable situations without embarrassment, and the best by 1980 were producing houses and other modest buildings, clad in traditional materials yet wholly without traditional detail, in a relaxed and unaffected manner that enriched their surroundings far more than their more pretentious predecessors. British architects were clearly quick learners.

Meanwhile the cleaning, repair and sensitive adaptation of historic buildings reached a level unprecedented in the history of this or any other country. This was the result of a combination of circumstances, of which the special impetus generated by European Architectural Heritage Year, 1975, was more a landmark than a cause. The three main causes were the stepping up of grants, starting with the Church of England's machinery for dealing with redundant churches (1968) and culminating in the National Heritage Memorial Fund (1980); the proliferation and growing expertise of the civic and preservation societies (there was now even a Thirties Society); and the widespread disillusion with the insensitive design, poor performance, and shoddy weathering of so many of the buildings of the boom years. By 1980 the country could begin to feel that in this sphere, as in some others, it was beginning to harvest the fruit of bitter experience.

Best of all, the Seventies saw the surrender of the cultural predominance of the London region. Not just in cathedral cities and pretty towns and villages where special trouble had been taken for some decades, but in the great industrial conurbations, there was an architectural and cultural renaissance. The black cities of the far north cleaned themselves up, planted trees, pedestrianised their commercial centres and began to produce new architecture worthy of their grand Victorian legacy.

Bolton Pedestrianisation of the Central Area (page 109)

19

CHAPTER TWO

Objectives

The Civic Trust went public, so to speak, in the summer of 1957. For a year or more Duncan Sandys, now Lord Duncan-Sandys, had been seeking the view of architects and planners, sounding out industrialists with a view to obtaining financial support, having a trust deed drawn up for approval by the Charity Commission, taking on first staff. An office was found and in July the Trust was launched publicly at a conference garden party held by invitation of the Archbishop of Canterbury at Lambeth Palace.

What was the point of the new Trust? The origins of the amenity movement, after all, go back at least a century and a half in Britain; many voluntary societies having a concern for different aspects of the environment already existed, some of very long-standing. Sandys had been made acutely aware, as Minister of Housing and Local Government, of the limitation of official action in matters of aesthetics and taste. Government, centrally or locally, cannot in a democracy move very far ahead of public opinion. It was borne in on him that certain things could be done more effectively by an independent agency than by a government department. The trouble was that, by and large, the existing associations were under-funded, under-staffed and very specialized in their concerns.

The central aim of the Trust, though it was not explicitly stated in those terms, was to effect a fundamental shift of public opinion; not itself to act as an arbiter of taste but to stimulate interest in, and concern for, environmental quality right across the board, in the belief that out of increased concern improved standards and better decisions would eventually flow. Although an opposition role, on occasions, was not forsworn, it seemed even more important in 1957, a quarter of a century ago, to make people aware of the positive possibilities open to them — to demonstrate the *results* of good design.

In practice, of course, carrot and stick both proved necessary. By the end of 1959 the Trust was involved heavily in the Piccadilly Circus Inquiry — the first planning case really to hit the headlines and become a *cause célèbre*. (One of the best descriptions of the Inquiry was by the incomparable Mollie Panter-Downes in her London Letter for the *New Yorker*.) But by then the Trust had also completed co-operative face-lifts for Magdalen Street in Norwich, and Burslem in Stoke-on-Trent. It had volunteer labour camps in many parts of the country, clearing abandoned war-time airfields and other eyesores. It was building up civic societies, holding conferences, making films . . . . Yet there was surely a

An indication of the range of work covered by the Trust's Awards – Almondell Footbridge, East Calder, Lothian (A1971); the Egyptian House, Penzance, Cornwall (H1975); Fort George, Inverness-shire, a massive archaeological rescue (A1971)

21

need somehow to make people more aware of the best work which was actually being done, sometimes even in their own locality? Why not a scheme of environmental awards?

The RIBA currently lists some 18 architectural award schemes in the United Kingdom (with another six international awards). Of these only four existed in the nineteen-fifties, three of them solely for housing. The Trust was thus breaking new ground when, in 1959 it announced plans for a new series of *environmental* awards. The essential aim of the scheme was to recognise a range of qualities at different levels. First, excellence of architecture, obviously, but no less the way in which buildings related to their setting, to other buildings and to the spaces between. Too often, even today, new buildings are conceived as ends in themselves rather than as contributors to an overall harmony.

But the Trust's Awards went further than this. They were applicable, not only to new buildings, but for creative excellence in the restoration and adaptation of old ones for new uses; for landscape improvements of every kind in town *and* countryside; for the *removal* of eyesores, from overhead wires to the reclamation of industrial dereliction. Furthermore, no limit was set to the *scale* of schemes submitted. Previously existing awards by and large went to projects of a certain size and importance. From the outset the Trust wished to recognise all those small examples of excellence which, incrementally and collectively, make such a far-reaching impact on our environment (think only, in the opposite direction, of the disastrous cumulative erosion of quality in our surroundings over the past thirty years by quite small individual acts — a picture window here, a garage extension there, a new shopfront across the way, a street widening down the road).

The Civic Trust's Awards have thus come to hold a special place in the still-proliferating galaxy of architectural and related award schemes. None other in the world embraces the same breadth of purpose and catholocity of entries; none other receives so many submissions. During the years since 1959, a staggering 13,738 entries have been received — notwithstanding that the only reward to the award winners is a certificate! The point has to be made here that honour is indeed paid to all those responsible for Award winning or commended schemes — owners and clients, architects and other designers, builders and craftsmen and, not infrequently, volunteer helpers; at the same time it is the *work itself* which receives the award and the essential purpose of that award is to make the work better known — to draw public attention to things which might otherwise go unnoticed; to offer the public standards by which to judge other changes in their locality; and thus to effect leverage upon public taste and strengthen the demand for higher standards in all other environmental work. Sometimes quality costs more, but by no means always; what is desirable is that we squeeze better value from whatever expenditure is going to be made anyway. And that is rarely impossible.

This objective underlay the machinery established for the administration of the scheme. If the awards were to have a local impact, they should as far as possible be organised locally. Who better to know what work has been going on in any particular area than the local planning authority? Often the authority will itself have played an important role in creating the right conditions for a scheme — by assisting the acquisition of land; by waiving routine criteria if appropriate; by integrating highway or other land use changes envisaged in the area; by itself forming part of a development consortium; and, of course, directly, in relation to its own housing and improvement schemes.

But would there be enough completed work to justify *annual* awards? Maybe every two or three years would be enough? But then the whole thing would lose impetus in the dead period between awards. Thus it was that for the first fifteen years of their life, the Civic Trust's Awards were made on a triennial basis in successive local authority areas — in the Counties, then the County Boroughs, for the third year in the London County Council area, and then back to the beginning again. The restructuring of local government in 1973–74 (and 1974–75 in Scotland) made this system obsolete. In fact, as a Civic Trust contribution to European Architectural Heritage Year, a one-off series of special Heritage Year Awards was made in 1975; thereafter, when the normal awards scheme was reintroduced, it was set up on a biennial basis, alternating between the Shire Counties, the Scottish Regions (excluding Edinburgh and Glasgow), Northern Ireland, the Isle of Man and Channel Islands in the first year; and Greater London, the Metropolitan Districts, Edinburgh and Glasgow in the second. These changes, taken in conjunction with some trial and error experimentation with categories of entry in earlier years, means that it is impossible, in a strict sense, to play the statistics game in relation to the number of awards received in particular areas over the years. Which is probably just as well.

In 1959 the Trust was but two years old; people were understandably a touch wary in their dealings with it. The RIBA demanded that all the assessors should be members of the Institute. A fair number of the local authorities written to did not even reply. And anyway, how did one get the existence of the thing known? In the event around 70 local authorities participated (no arrangements could be made for other areas, which led to confusion and ill feeling); the number of entries was 669; there was no check upon the verdict of the assessors whose decisions, all arrived at separately, were accepted long-range. A duplicated note made the results — of which, in some cases, the less said the better — known to the press.

But it was a beginning. Local authority participation has for long been complete. By comparison with those early days the machinery which has now been established may seem even a little heavy-handed; it is upon these procedures, however, that the present authority of the results rests.

From the outset assessors were faced with difficult problems of comparability. How do you judge the removal of a slagheap against the pedestrianisation of a busy street or a housing project of many hectares? And to what extent is it right — or possible — to seek to apply the same qualitative standards everywhere, regardless of local circumstances? On the one hand it may seem sensible to allow a measure of flexibility — but on the other it is clearly inequitable to those submitting if standards are allowed to diverge too far.

These are some of the problems of judgement which arise. Others exist, an abbreviation of the Trust's guidance notes to assessors is given on page 138.

So far so good, but guidance of this kind is only a beginning. A number of procedures follow, which are designed to lead towards a reasonable consistency in the results. Assessors' recommendations are forwarded to London and put on show. Assessors attend this exhibition, study standards and debate them with their fellows, and may wish to amend their initial recommendations accordingly. For a good many years now a second-tier 'Awards Panel' composed of Past Presidents or similarly distinguished representatives from the

RIBA, the Royal Town Planning Institute, and the Landscape Institute, has additionally sought to bring assessors' recommendations into a national focus. The practice is that the Awards Panel meets to form a preliminary view, express doubts, ask for more information; the main body of assessors then assemble in London, the Panel's views are put to them, and assessors, with their greater weight of local knowledge, can respond as they think fit; the Panel then meets a second time for further consideration of the submissions — perhaps to discuss them with the assessors concerned — before finally deciding upon the year's awards and commendations.

There is one further way in which the procedure is strengthened. Since 1975 assessors have been flanked on their rounds by two 'local advisers' — one from the planning department concerned and one from the amenity society world. The essential purpose of the advisers is to ensure, from their local knowledge, that there are no background facts to any particular submission of which the assessor — who will have come from another part of the country — is unaware. To learn that intense local controversy surrounded the demolition of some old almshouses before a new building arose on the site, will not necessarily change his view that the latter merits an award — but he should be aware of all such matters before forming his view.

It will be seen, therefore, that a Civic Trust Award represents quite a complex consensus judgement, resulting from an often intense dialogue conducted at a number of different levels between a wide range of interests. It is not fanciful to see in the assessment process itself an educational spin-off of some value. Assessors have frequently admitted how valuable they have found it to have a look at things with a rather different eye; they and their 'advisers' have time and again commented on what they have learned from one another. An intangible benefit this, but, grossed up over the years (in all, many hundreds of people have been involved in the assessing process), it seems likely that horizons have been stretched for an important sector of those most closely concerned with environmental matters.

The Trust's army of assessors reached its peak in 1975 when, altogether, some 470 assessors and advisers were on the march. In the autumn of 1972 the Trust had been requested by the Department of the Environment to administer the UK campaign for European Architectural Heritage Year 1975 — the second of the Council of Europe's major environmental initiatives. As a contribution to the campaign, the Trust decided to make a special series of Heritage Year Awards. These differed from the normal awards in several respects. They were concerned only with historic buildings and areas; they embraced interior restoration work as well as exterior; there was no limitation of awards — that is to say, anything which reached a certain standard was considered award-worthy. *And,* the whole of the UK was to be covered in one year.

In some ways, the operation proved a continuing nightmare. To fit the timetable to the Heritage Year programme as a whole, judging had to take place during the winter. Many assessors faced appalling conditions. One, snowbound in the north of Scotland, was forced to hire a helicopter to get to an entry on one of the islands (and wrote apologetically; 'I am sorry about the expense'). The Trust became concerned, in so large an exercise, about consistency of standards and decided to have *all* submissions sent to London for examination. The sheer bulk of nearly 1,400 large brown paper parcels in an office already overcrowded by additional Heritage Year staff, created a situation which seared all those directly concerned. At the same time, the national economy lurched and inflation really took off. The Trust ended up with a deficit of £20,000.

Nonetheless, in terms of its objectives, the operation proved a huge success. 285 Awards were made. The main winners, together with the recipients of a series of additional awards for 'continuing performance' received their awards — a specially designed medal by Louis Osman, presented by the Hon. Company of Goldsmiths — from HRH the Duke of Edinburgh at an impressive ceremony in the Waterloo Chamber of Windsor Castle. The Trust's submission of thirteen main entries to the Council of Europe's international award scheme for the year resulted in eleven awards — a far higher number than that received by any other participating country. And the substantial printed report on the results received wide praise. Two typical comments:

> . . . the most comprehensive and easiest available single source of reference on high quality conservation in Britain that we are likely to possess for a long time to come.

Building, 27 June 1975

> For the Civic Trust to embark upon the awesome task of administering a scheme requiring the co-ordination of 470 people and the assessment of 1,377 projects throughout the length and breadth of Britain in order to produce 285 awards 'to highlight, and to honour, practical conservation work which has furthered the objectives of European Architectural Heritage Year' is an achievement worthy of an award itself.
>
> The end-product of all the hard work is an excellent report, which does not deserve a place on every bookshelf where it may never be read, but rather a place on every planner's and councillor's bedside table, where it may be a constant source of inspiration.

MICHAEL HANSON, *Municipal Journal,* 27 June 1975

This marked the end of a whole phase of the Awards scheme. Apart from the losses incurred by the Heritage Year campaign, the Trust now found itself, like everyone else, hard hit by galloping inflation. Unfortunately, charities and voluntary organisations have no means of passing on rising costs to their consumers. The Trust, receiving no government grant towards its general funds, found its spending power declining steadily — to the point where it was in fact no more than half the level in 1957. The Trustees regretfully felt bound to cut from the programme the Trust's most expensive single activity — the Awards scheme.

It was for this reason that the continuity of the scheme's twenty-two years of existence suffered a break of nearly two years after 1975. Salvation came in the form of commercial sponsorship — first from Messrs. Bass Limited and then from the Midland Bank. Thanks to their generosity, and now to The Grosvenor Estate and MEPC Limited, the Awards were once more in full swing in 1978 (with an increased period of eligibility to take account of the break), each sponsor supporting the scheme for one two-year cycle. The Trust owes them a great debt of gratitude.

What then has it all amounted to? To what extent has the scheme achieved the objectives aimed at nearly a quarter of a century ago? These things can never be quantified. For the record, between 1959 and 1981, 13,738 submissions were received, 1,071 awards were made and 1,709 schemes were commended. No fewer than 500 assessors of distinction gave their time and expertise to the appraisal of entries.

Sometimes, it has been possible to trace some direct knock-on effect of the scheme. Architects have received commissions on the strength of award-winning entries. Local authority committees, in trouble for some 'daring' development they have sponsored, have found their position strengthened by receipt of a Civic Trust Award. A note of reservation in connection with the first phase of a big scheme has borne fruit in the execution of subsequent phases. And so on.

And standards generally? 'Civic Trust Awards are not easy to come by. Since 1959, when the annual award scheme was started, the Trust has, by setting high standards and rigorously keeping to them, ensured that an award is something to be coveted' wrote the *Estates Gazette* in 1975. It is beyond doubt that design standards are incomparably higher today than they were in 1959 (a fact which is reflected in the criteria applied to submissions; certain things which demanded a public pat on the back fifteen or twenty years ago can now to some extent be taken for granted and no longer figure among the annual results unless they are also pace-setters in another way). It could be claimed that more good development has taken place in Britain over the past twenty years than during the previous half century. But that does not invalidate the fact that over the same period more damage has been wrought to the character of our towns than in any equivalent period in the past. Public opinion is far more alert to what we could and should be doing — but we are not yet doing it. We have yet to achieve that minimum level of environmental good manners to which we are entitled in all the workaday changes that are inevitable in our surroundings.

Wrote *The Architect* in April 1973: 'the report of the annual Civic Trust Awards represents in some ways a yearly compendium of hope for our surroundings. When one's senses are daily bombarded with ugliness and destruction it is very easy to lose sight of the fact that there are still many good works being done around the country.'

The need to point the way, in other words, is as great as ever. Whatever environmental challenges we face in the future, they are unlikely to repeat those of the past two decades. The daunting problems of the inner city, the continuing pressures upon land, the effects of the micro-chip upon traditional patterns of living — these alone will tax our ingenuity and determination to the full. Nonetheless, we may take courage from the pages which follow. They show that it is within our power dramatically to reshape the physical fabric of Britain for the better — if only we choose to do so.

CHAPTER THREE

A Stroll among the Winners

Three things must be said at the outset. First, that out of the 2780 projects that received awards and commendations in the period under review it has only been possible to illustrate 173 in this book — 1 in 16. So this can only be a personal and arbitrary choice and a tiny sample of an output of good work every bit as remarkable for its quantity as its quality. Second, that the awards and commendations cannot claim to represent the Best of British Architecture between 1957 and 1982. A few brilliant architects never took part, some local authorities put less effort than others into promoting the scheme, some good buildings were not submitted for this reason or that. Third, that the categories which follow, and the places which get special attention, are equally arbitrary. Many projects belong in more than one category or are hard to fit into any. All outlines are fuzzy. This is a contemplative stroll through the world we have been building around us in Britain in this last quarter-century, not a series of raids on separate strongpoints.

Of course the scheme took a bit of time to get into its stride. Even in 1960, a year of important new buildings, assessors were prepared to salute the skimpiest of commercial development in a city as famous as Canterbury, and to regard the replacement of a jolly Edwardian shopfront or a glum police station as improvements, however affected or commonplace the result. Full Awards, for example, went to the Borough Engineer's eight-storey flats in Kirkcaldy (1960) and to some bleak brick blocks in Scunthorpe (1959). But soon, great things began to happen.

Scunthorpe (left), Kirkcaldy ▷
(right)

The Severn Bridge (page 31)

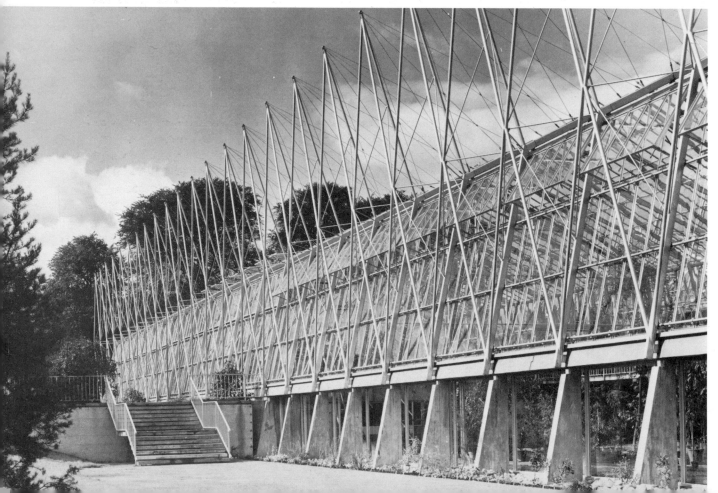

St Patrick's Church, Strabane, Co Tyrone

Singletons

It was never the purpose of this scheme to compete with the RIBA's own awards in seeking out individual or isolated masterpieces. But all through its history assessors found a few hard to resist — the Severn Bridge, for example (A 1968), functionalism *In excelsis,* once described by Sir Misha Black as 'the most beautiful artefact of the 20th century' (yet fatally compromised as an object in space by the presence alongside it of a parody in the shape of the cross-Severn power line). Power stations, a few showpiece factories on greenfield sites, new universities in romantic landscapes and of course cathedrals, churches and crematoria share this attribute of gathering their surroundings about them in a new synthesis. Some of these we shall meet later in their proper places. But a few have seemed worth singling out at this stage, if only because they resist classification. In the Royal Botanic Garden in Edinburgh are two structures by architects of the old Ministry of Works, whose great traditions going back to Wren are now buried, typically of our time, in the featureless and futureless initials DOE and PSA. In fact the master architect was George Pearce and the engineer Francis Whalley. The herbarium and botanical library (A 1966) is faintly neo-classic in the manner of Soane, perhaps to reflect Mathieson's 1858 Palm House. The other building (A 1969), laid out to link the

Herbarium and Botanical Library (top) and Exhibition Plant Houses, Edinburgh

*Elephant and Rhinoceros
Pavilion, London Zoo*

two, is a long greenhouse full of fascinating, uncluttered, interior landscapes, each a work of art — a building worthy to stand in the succession going back to Paxton and Burton, yet having a filigree spider's-web delicacy reminiscent of the mysterious space-age installations one finds in the windy landscape west of Cambridge. Could anything be in stronger contrast, eloquent of the versatility of modern architecture, than the Elephant House at the London Zoo (C 1967); this huddle of massive pachydermatous shapes, gathered together like their inmates round a waterhole, is at the other extreme of architectural expression. A conspicuous example of the Zoological Society's consistent policy of enlightened planning and patronage, its roughly circular shape and monumental character makes it the natural centre-piece that the Zoo's casually assembled buildings had hitherto lacked.

Finally, two Celtic hill-top churches, both of which not only dramatise their surrounding landscapes but confer on them an indefinable 'otherness.' One stands high on windy pastures near Strabane in County Tyrone, a massive granite hexagon rising to forty-two square stained-glass windows in deeply recessed metal-faced mullions (A 1971). The other crowns the centre of the New Town of East Kilbride on the edge of Glasgow (A 1965).

I shall not often quote an assessor's citation, but this one by E. W. Hall cannot be bettered—

St Bride's Church and Presbytery, East Kilbride

'This most distinguished building enriches by its power and strength of character the whole town centre of East Kilbride and must be considered one of the most notable buildings completed in Scotland in recent years.

The church, massive in itself and strangely reminiscent of the Scottish castle, attains a greater dominance over the surroundings by its siting prominently on rising ground surrounded by fine trees. The campanile, meticulously sited at the edge of the slope, is a landmark for the district.

The church building is designed with stout load-bearing walls of a rough red brick and, using every device of the bricklayer's craft, conveys both timelessness and the eternal joy of building. These qualities, more often found in historic buildings, are rare in modern work and are of immense value in the setting of a New Town such as East Kilbride. Valuable also is the great restraint in limiting the choice of materials.

Arriving at the entrance piazza, the fortress-like enclosure of the church with its almost secret entrances and absence of window openings, anticipates perfectly the mystery and awe of the interior.'

No man is an island, and no building is independent of its surroundings, with which it holds two-way converse fascinating to analyse. It is a short step from these landscape-transforming buildings to a group of projects in which the landscape dominates and the works of man subserve it.

Landscape

We must face it that our century is not going to measure up to the last three in the history of the landscape. A population multiplied nearly tenfold over that span, requiring not only new and more spacious cities but all the supporting utilities — power, water, transportation, recreation — would alone have seen to that. Moreover the landowners who created the lowland landscape have either disappeared or lost the incentive of believing that their heirs will inherit their handiwork; the rural crafts that turned out farm buildings and equipment organically related to the land that carried them have been superseded by industrial products with no such relationship; the elms have gone and with them the camouflage they provided for all our contemporary clutter — not to mention the park-like prospects that so astonished visitors; and perhaps most damaging of all, we have as a result of these upheavals lost the philosophy of landscape as a perfect marriage of utility and beauty within which every individual could work intuitively: we are fumbling in the dark.

So it is mitigation, concealment and restoration rather than new creation that we are nowadays concerned with, and the awards reflect this. This does not mean that nobody is planting : many landowners, farmers and conservationist groups are, and would not expect an award for it. Typical is Mr Roper of Lenborough near Buckingham who did receive a 1978 Award for planting no less than 5,500 trees in every odd corner of his previously elm-studded thousand-acre mixed farm. Nearby, the new city of Milton Keynes has been stuffing its wide spaces with saplings as liberally as any prince of the *Grand Siècle*. But much of the new planting is compensatory or camouflage. The same goes of

Mr Roper's farm where over 5,500 trees have been planted

Some of the main species planted on the 39 sites
Beech
Birch
Elm
European Larch
Field Maple
Hawthorn
Leyland Cypress
Lime
Norway Maple
Oak
Plane
Poplar
Rowan
Sycamore
Wild Cherry
Wildcrab
Willow (a variety)
Whitebeam

course for the laborious task of clearing up the wastelands of the Industrial Revolution, particularly the tips and scars of mineral extraction. This may be a moral imperative : it is not invariably a scenic improvement. Bland down-like contours do not marry with the rugosities of the North and West. Who would want to raze the white china-clay peaks of St. Austell? But when the scale is great enough and the long haul is master-minded by people of vision the final effect can be spectacular. The greening of Stoke-on-Trent (A 1969/72), said to have had more industrial wasteland within its boundaries than any other English town, is probably the most extensive single effort of this kind (though the Lower Swansea Valley has possibly posed even greater problems). But undoubtedly the most dramatic is the removal of the huge black tips that used to overhang the south side of the slate-quarrying village of Ballachulish at the far end of Glencoe (A 1980). Green slopes and 80,000 young trees have worked an almost miraculous transformation.

Mineral extraction will always be the most devastating blow for the landscape to absorb. Other new demands — afforestation, water-works, motorways — can be opportunities, water-works most of all. These can range from total concealment, as with the underground pumping station on the shore of Ullswater (A 1971), to total transformation as with the great Llyn Celyn (Trywern) reservoir in North Wales (C 1968). This, at any rate at high water, is surely a landscape gain; but it was a human tragedy to the inhabitants of the drowned valley, as is properly recorded by the charmingly designed stone chapel at the water's edge (A 1971) recording the names of those buried beside the submerged church. Somewhere between these extreme cases is the beautifully handled small hydro-electric scheme at Felin·Newydd near Aberystwyth (A 1962). Deep down

Lee Abbey Farm, Linton, Devon (A 1971)

Hanley Forest Park, Stoke-on-Trent

37

*Reservoir and Chapel, Llyn Celyn (Trywern), North Wales (top);
Ullswater Pumping Station, Cumbria*

Opposite page
*Bridges, Heads of the Valley Road, A465, Gwent (top);
The A40 between Monmouth and Symonds Yat, Herefordshire*

in the quiet, wooded Rheidol gorge the new mirror-smooth lake ends in a prettily curving weir, and picnic spots have been unobtrusively provided. There are no overhead power lines, but except when the lake level is unusually high the black line of the concrete dam is an intrusion.

The new roads have by and large been less brutal visually than the railways of the last century. This particularly applies where the authorities have been content with Class A double-tracking rather than the full motorway treatment. Nothing could be more delightful than the truly improved A40 in the Wye Valley between Monmouth and Symonds Yat (C 1971), its grand curves and terraced carriageways in perfect sympathy with the winding river and the rounded wooded hills. And the best of the road bridges, as for example the outstandingly elegant 'Heads of the Valleys' bridges in Gwent (A 1968), are not unworthy successors, in their lean athletic way, to the tremendous viaducts of the past.

Last and newest demand upon the land is mass recreation. A caravan site on the Firth of Forth (A 1968) shows that even this invasion can be handled. Six-foot-high banks of buckthorn divide it into a dozen separate free-shaped enclosures, giving campers some privacy and binding the whole into the landscape. Compared with this most intractable of problems, permanent holiday buildings, given the right designer, are easy. Herodsfoot, a Forestry Commission village in Cornwall (A 1978) perches, seemingly at random, on the foundations of abandoned mine buildings or is ledged into the valley hillside. At a higher level of sophistication and permanence is the Wildfowl Trust visitor's building (A 1980), tucked into the wooded slope below Arundel Castle and overlooking the meres and water-meadows of the Arun Valley floor. With this carefully composed group we are back in the realm of architecture.

*Caravan Site at Yellowcraig
on the Firth of Forth, Scotland*

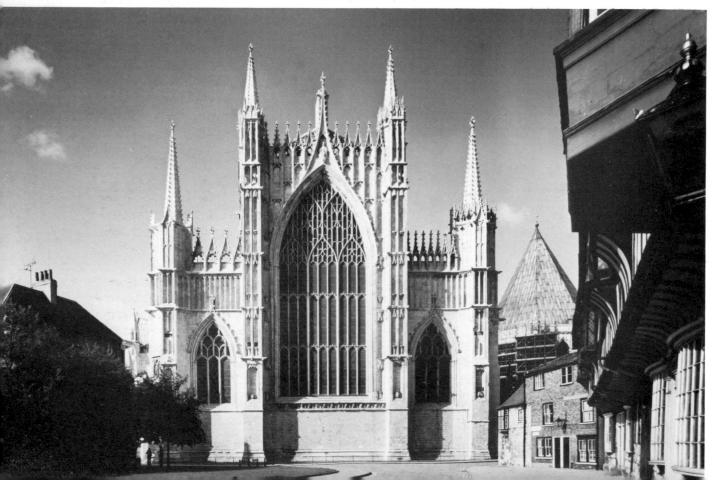

Restorations and Conversions

It is always a pity to have to isolate 'conservation' since it is a spectrum stretching from running repairs to the tactful insertion of new buildings into old settings. At one end it shades off into normal maintenance, at the other into all architecture. The 1975 Heritage Awards cut it up into three, but here we need be less systematic. One thing is clear. A hundred years ago our landscape was far better, but our cities and towns were far worse. We should not be beguiled by Victorian photographs of empty cobbled streets into supposing otherwise. Apart from the appalling slums, the appalling pollution and the abrogation of planning and urban design, the neglect or misuse of the heritage (except for the churches against whose ill-treatment William Morris protested so passionately) was as total as it always had been — only more serious because there was more of it. 18th century frontages if not destroyed were re-fenestrated, 19th century stucco was left to peel or painted battleship grey, country towns and villages were in the last stages of picturesque decay. Taste in past styles of architecture was highly selective and only possessed at all by a tiny group of aesthetes.

We celebrate in this section an extraordinary cultural revolution. We now love everything, agonise over the loss of old buildings of even mediocre quality, and have imposed the language, not to say the jargon, of conservation on even the most philistine of local authorities, developers and owners. Its practice has become so universal and so well-documented that what follows has to be proportionally the smallest sample of all — and perhaps the most personal. It seems fitting to start with York and Lancaster, and first with the rescue of the sinking Minster (H 1975) in a superb feat of engineering made possible by the raising of £2 million mainly in Yorkshire itself. The photographs of the restored east end show that it was an environmental gain as well, though this is only a fraction of the renewal of the walled city inspired by a dedicated York Civic Trust and a converted City Council. The clean-up and the elegant modern extension of the Theatre Royal, previously considered a hideosity, is only one of several distinguished examples (A 1969), but it deserves a pause in every tourist's itinerary because the extension, while properly subservient to its stodgy Gothic neighbour, is by far the best 20th century building within the walls and in its gracefulness, transparency and dramatic use of interior space exemplifies what modern architecture was all about. In Lancaster there has been the rescue of the pretty little Music Room (C 1978), with its rather French facade and its beautiful internal plaster work, of which Pevsner had written in 1969 'it is now so decayed that there can be no hope of saving it.' On a larger canvas, Lancaster's pedestrianised shopping street is one of the best, and the office development (A 1978) which now spreads across the whole middle distance of the view of the castle from across the Lune witnesses to the tireless efforts of all concerned, not least the consultant recommended by the Royal Fine Art Commission, to get it right.

To mention here these two new university cities and not a third, Norwich, may seem perverse, but the Norwich achievement is so outstanding that it will later have a paragraph to itself. However while in East Anglia two triumphs must be recorded, the Maltings at Snape (A 1968) a masterly conversion familiar to many as the pleasantest concert hall in England, and the less familiar conversion of the Corn Exchange in Sudbury (A 1971) into a cheerful and airy public library. The Suffolk vernacular of Snape and the Victorian baroque of Sudbury,

Music Room, Lancaster

The East End of York Minster, repaired, repaved and cleared of traffic

St. Nicholas Church, Bristol

unusual for its date, are equally sympathetically handled. The retention of this latter key building greatly enhances the central space of this colourful and splendidly maintained market town, even though St. Peter's great church that dominates the market place has had to be closed. Among rural regions East Anglia is unique in the number of its empty churches, some of them in lonely fields where once stood thriving villages depopulated by the Black Death or by the decline of the wool trade. Historic cities like York and Norwich, Bristol and Ipswich, with clusters of Gothic churches in their medieval centres now equally depopulated, have a similar problem. The Church of England's Pastoral Measure procedure has saved a great many, either by conversion to some other use or, where this seemed impracticable or undesirable, by preservation in the hands of the Redundant Churches Fund. In Bristol the 18th century St. Nicholas Church (H 1975), built over a beautiful medieval crypt and with an important spire, having been reduced to a shell in the War, was taken over by the City Council and delightfully converted into a museum of local history and church art, which houses, *inter alia,* Hogarth's great altarpiece from St. Mary Redcliffe. The light and airy interior has exactly the right feel, and the vaulted crypt, restored and romantically lit, has been rightly kept empty.

But undoubtedly the most extensive and satisfying re-creation of a vernacular tradition is in the lowlands of Scotland. This is partly because harled walls and contrasting painted architraves can be done over more easily than old brick and stone and marry more easily with modern materials. The National Trust for Scotland's delightful restorations in the fishing towns and villages of East Fife, as at Pittenweem (A 1965) and St. Monance (page 46) are the best-known examples; but the central area at Jedburgh (A 1978), where the buildings are

Piece Hall, Halifax (page 52)

Opposite page
Central Market Building Covent Garden, London (page 52)

Makerstoun House, Kelso

Opposite
The Maltings, Snape (top); St Monance, Fife, one of the earliest towns to benefit from the National Trust for Scotland's 'Little Houses' scheme

Home Farm Buildings, Culzean

on a grander and more urban scale, is equally distinguished, and must be a delight to live in as it is to visit. Not far away, on the banks of the Tweed near Kelso, is Makerstoun House (H 1975), a remarkable example of what has just been said about harling. Who, seeing this William Adam facade of 1714, could imagine what the house looked like in its Victorian stone casing after it was gutted by fire in 1970? This was private enterprise at its best. But undoubtedly the most impressive conversion in Scotland is on the Ayrshire coast. Culzean is Robert Adam's grandest castle, spectacularly situated on the rocky edge of the Atlantic. Given to the National Trust by Lord Ailsa in 1945, its 531 acres were in 1969 declared Scotland's first country park, and it was soon receiving visitors at the rate of over 250,000 a year. To accommodate them the Trust's consultant advised against a new building and proposed the reconstruction and conversion of Adam's very Scottish, very rational yet at the same time very romantic Home Farm buildings of 1777. The result is the rescue and manifest improvement of a unique complex for which no other use could have been so appropriate (H 1975). The whole estate provides, moreover, a useful exemplar of consortium working in the management agreements made between the Trust, Ayr County Council and the Town Council of Ayr and Kilmarnock, the then planning authorities and their successors.

We move from the wild Atlantic to the snuggest of Cotswold valleys. On the green bank of the rushing Windrush at Minster Lovell in Oxfordshire (H 1975) there hides a Centre for Advanced Studies created by major extension of an old house and barns. The use of long glazed ranges, deeply recessed into timber mullions under stone roofs, recalls the late 19th as well as the early 16th centuries, and the linkage of old and new is handled with consummate naturalness.

The Corn Exchange, Sudbury Suffolk (page 43-4)

This is a minor masterpiece and it is sad that from the lane the passer-by can only see its properly blank back wall. It is interesting to compare this deeply traditional extension by a young architect with the work of an older generation in a commuters' village near Exeter. Winslade Manor (A 1980) stands high on a spacious greensward — a mid-Victorian stucco block, rather thinly detailed and in architectural quality no match for the new wing. Yet this strongly modelled and expansive extension is kept low enough not to compete and demonstrates that a modernist classic can be as restrained as any other.

The cleaned and restored Royal Courts of Justice, London (H 1975)

And so to London and two more rescues of the eclectic work of John Nash. Ulster Terrace (H 1975) is one of the last and least flamboyant pieces of his Regent's Park scenery, so skin-deep that it was reckoned in the forties that it would all have to go the way of Regent Street. All the terraces have needed rebuilding behind the facades, some even preceded by total demolition. Like Nash himself, nobody thought the look of the backs mattered much; but how he would have enjoyed this faintly Islamic and highly ingenious *jeu d'esprit!* (page 10). I am not sure he would have approved the Coutts glass-house in the Strand so much (A 1979), handsome of its kind though this cautious version of the fashionable American atrium undoubtedly is. having applauded the quixotic decision to prop up the crumbling facades and rebuild totally behind them he would surely have wished to have his centre-piece restored and seen as a

One of the many terraces restored by the Greater London Council, Foxley Road, Lambeth

Fitzroy Road, Camden

solecism the chopping off of his most important elevation in mid-career.

However, in London achievement in conservation does not rest on such showpieces, but on the rehabilitation of countless Georgian and Victorian terraces and squares made possible by Government grants, the growth of housing associations and the initiative of enlightened Councils, of whom the LCC/GLC, Lambeth and Islington deserve special mention. Only one illustration can here be given of vast and beneficent urban transformation. Fitzroy Road is a wide street of handsome early Victorian villas on the eastern fringes of Primrose Hill. In their midst is Hopkinson's monumentally pedimented stock-brick factory of 1866 which at one time turned out 800 pianos a day. It has converted superbly into 48 dwellings of higher standard, according to the Council, than would have been the case with redevelopment, and at a rather lower cost. Aspects can be criticised : the building's thickness and sense of weight has encouraged the rather heavy-handed detailing of pergolas and footways, and the bottom-hung inward-opening windows make it impossible ever to lean out and talk to a friend below. But the building's new lease of life (the full 60 years) was richly deserved, and enhances its neighbourhood (A 1981).

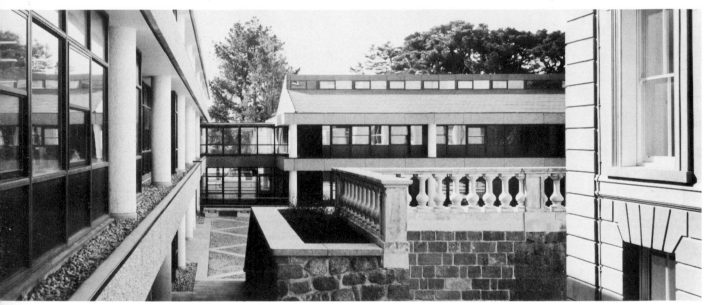

Extension to the Theatre Royal, York (page 43) (top left); The Centre for Advanced Studies, Minster Lovell, Oxfordshire (page 47) (top right); Winslade Manor, Exeter (page 48) (centre); Coutts Bank, Strand, London (page 48)

Industrial Archaeology

This rather pretentious phrase is useful to distinguish an aspect of conservation which only differs from the rest in that it always involves a change of use, generally from organised work to organised leisure, and it is this radical change which produces its special problems. The first and earliest example is no problem but pure delight. Chesterton Windmill in Warwickshire (H 1975), built in 1632 by an ingenious landowner who was clearly an admirer and patron of Inigo Jones and his associates, is unique in Europe (there is an inferior copy on Rhode Island) and the second oldest to survive in England. Jones, who built 'the finest barn in Europe' in Covent Garden has here inspired the finest windmill, which is also incidentally a highly sophisticated piece of masonry. As to Covent Garden, the Market Building restoration and conversion (A 1981) is the culmination of a long and contentious story, and there are those who puritanically abhor the high rents the GLC has had to demand to recoup its £2½ million expenditure, and the consequent influx into this previously raffish and plebeian enclave of chic boutiques and tourist traps. But in architectural terms it is a triumph and seems to have lifted the whole building and its environ- ment on to a higher plane, a plane, incidentally, which neither Fowler in 1827 nor Cubitt in 1875, seeing their problem in purely practical terms, had ever contemplated for it.

With Ironbridge and Coalbrookdale (A 1978, C 1980) we are in an altogether more serious environment — no less than the birthplace, if there is any single one, of the Industrial Revolution. Slipping down into the thickly wooded Severn gorge at Coalport, you can't miss the hugely rotund bottle kilns of the China Works — visual predecessors of the red cooling towers at the other end of the gorge. Like all the displays initiated by the Ironbridge Gorge Museum Trust, the museum design is impeccable (C 1978). The bridgeheads of the Iron Bridge Itself and the backcloth village have been re-paved and re-bollarded and gener- ally refurbished, as has the Great Warehouse in Coalbrookdale, now housing the Museum of Iron, an 1838 gabled building with a charming clock turret, cleaned and cleared of clutter and its millponds and footbridge restored (C 1980). In complete stylistic contrast is the castellated and heavily buttressed Severn Warehouse, now an Interpretation Centre (A 1978), just west of Ironbridge, with a romantic peep back at the Bridge itself. Westward again we pass the carefully landscaped and beautifully timbered riverside park created by Telford New Town in mitigation of the hotly contested CEGB decision to site a new power station in the gorge (C 1978). In fact this is so much better than the reckless old one, and looms up so mysteriously behind the trees, that no penance was needed. This whole immensely popular tourist attraction is now almost comically tasteful, when one considers what it commemorates.

Contemporary with these epoch-making developments in the Severn gorge were the earliest canals. Of the original 3900 miles of canal in the UK, 2000 miles are still navigable and are of course the greatest single example of conver- sion from industrial to recreational use. Several examples of the careful work of the British Waterways Board, of riparian authorities and of Canal Trusts in restoring locks, bridges, machinery, towpaths and canal buildings have had Awards and Commendations. I illustrate the lock staircase at Bingley (H 1975) as an excellent no-nonsense job in a rural setting, and at the other extreme the transformation of a characteristic canal scene in the heart of Birmingham

Chesterton Windmill, Warwickshire

51

Bingley Locks, Yorkshire

(A 1969) (the central island is seen in both photographs). This derelict area, previously concealed from public view, is now the busy heart of the canal fun scene, with a metropolitan air of centrality enhanced by tall flats and other new buildings, which, unremarkable in themselves, seem to gain in attraction by reflection. Brightly painted narrow boats, spruced-up impedimenta and the new Longboat pub give you a reassuring sense of arrival. But the reader must make his own assessment of what we have gained and lost. Romantics who mourn the silent, fog-shrouded, melancholy past may be comforted to know that many such atmospheric scenes survive, in Birmingham as elsewhere. I would only plead that when we do get at them we prettify them as little as possible.

In the great Piece Hall at Halifax (A 1979) there has been no prettification at all. Canal engineers played some part in the design of this masterly market building, opened with a great firework display and procession in 1779 and re-opened with an open-air ball attended by 1500 people on a cloudless summer evening in 1976. Seen from inside the great courtyard, the way the slope has been managed is admirable. To the east the restored spire of the Square Chapel soars dizzily against the backcloth of the moors, and a few ham-fisted office blocks that poke up to the west will, one hopes, one day be demolished. Piece Hall is the most astonishing recovery of twentieth century conservation in Britain.

The Wharfage/Tontine Hill, Ironbridge (top left); Museum of Iron, Coalbrookdale (top right); The Severn Wharf, Interpretation Centre, Ironbridge (bottom left); The Coalport China Works Museum (bottom right)

Opposite page
Kingston Row & James Brindley Walk, Birmingham, before and after

Skilful Knitting

At a certain point in the spectrum the old building, modified as may be by
conversion and addition, ceases to predominate, the new is entitled to its own
identity and we are in the realm of infill — the knitting together into a single
composition of old and new. Two examples from the North, neither of which
resort at all to pastiche, admirably demonstrate the skill. The first is the new
health centre in the large Yorkshire village of Pocklington (A 1971), which lies
below the Wolds midway between York and Hull. Its materials are in sympathy
with the liver-coloured bricks and warm red pantiles of the region (though one
misses the chimneys) and well-maintained wooden bay-windows, while not
themselves a vernacular feature, prevent a too insistent horizontality. The
second, a Branch Library on a corner site in the prosperous Newcastle suburb
of Jesmond (A 1963), is a properly more sophisticated and more urban design,
but it also carefully respects the eaves line of the adjacent Victorian terraces. By
contrast, two examples from the South illustrate the different problem of joining
and making some new contribution to the usual mixed bunch of street faces.
The little bookshop in Holywell, Oxford (A 1972), sits back modestly and belies
its complex and remarkably spacious interior; the fun is all at the back, where
the building turns out to contain college rooms and to make an intriguing

King William Street Redevelopment, Blackburn (page 61) (top); Mitre House Development, Lancaster (page 43)

contribution to the innermost recesses of Wadham. The Midland Bank extension (A 1972) close to the Cross where the four Roman roads of Gloucester meet is a simpler problem but joins a more variegated and noisy party. Its calm, quiet statement and generous proportions are just about the best thing in the street.

My last pair of street faces are in London where of course the scale is larger still. One is for a French client, the other for a German. The Banque Nationale de Paris in the City (A 1979) joins a pompous assemblage of 19th and 20th century edifices and pays them the compliment of wearing the regulation costume of columns and entablature, but does so in a witty and wholly modern way that is nevertheless entirely serious. The scale is appropriately grand. The other is in Belgravia, turning an oblique angle from Chesham Place to join the German Embassy in Belgrave Square (A 1979). In its now rather old-fashioned way, it does so with skill and panache. One's only fear is whether its white concrete will stay as fresh as the adjacent painted stucco. Round the corner in Lowndes Street, for example, is a block of flats (C 1964) whose black and white bricks have done so admirably. Its flashy 1964 modernity, as the Assessor remarked, by no means disqualifies it for the opulent Belgravian scene.

A great deal of urban infill in recent years has been in depth: modest gaps in street frontages have been exploited to give access to untold wonders behind the scenes, where no resemblance to living persons is intended — or

St George's Street Development, Winchester

necessary. This is another subject. But the next three examples show insertions that are more than skin-deep visually and yet take care to respond to the old scale and texture. The Lanes in Brighton (A 1966), with its Sussex tile hanging and Brighton bay windows, is by now a cherished part of anybody's day excursion. This souk-like huddle of small shops was one of the first to recognise the need to compress the customers in order to impress an atmosphere of commercial success. Inevitably less well known, but an equally happy beneficiary of the removal of the motor-car, is the main street of old Harlow (A 1971), where new and old are unified not by imitation but by the general use of Essex white plaster and sensible landscaping. The new shops at Winchester (A 1965) are the bright spot of a central renewal area that contrasts rather bleakly with the snug medieval core of the city. One terrace is carefully related to a handsome Queen Anne house on the corner; the other is correctly quite different, with concrete frame and brick panels, yet equally nicely scaled, with a delicacy of touch characteristic of its architects. Sixteen years later, the same quality is evident in an entirely different inner-London setting. This is 'Hobhouse Court' (A 1981), named after the first Commissioner to the Crown Estate in 1834. It is the creation not of a building but of a space, by the selective removal of the accretions that in London (unlike Paris, where ever since the 17th century the Roman *cortile* has been the model) have choked up the backs of so many handsome

*Brighton Square, The Lanes,
Brighton*

The Economist Development,
St James's Street, London

terraces. In this case, just west of the National Gallery, the new space links dignified Suffolk Street with workaday Whitcombe Street via two little tunnels and a charming and impeccably detailed secret courtyard furnished with two flourishing young plane-trees. Brown brick and pale cream stucco, York paving and granite setts, are the pairs of materials that properly monopolise the scene, and there is a cheering sense of previously decayed old structures brought back to healthy life. The contrast with the horrific Royal Trafalgar Hotel across the way is worth noting. Not far away, one can see a similar but much larger problem solved in the manner of the sixties by total redevelopment. The designers of the Economist development (C 1967), inventors of Brutalism, are here on their best behaviour, using gentlemanly materials, keeping to the street height in St. James's Street but going higher, with surprising changes of module, for the blocks of offices and flats in the background. But the little-used 'piazza' seems scarcely worth the removal of the supporting buildings that Boodles Club had always had. Ten years later the recourse to deeper office plans would probably have suggested a conventional perimeter development.

Taking out whole blocks of 'obsolete' central city property and replacing

60

them with scaled-up shopping centres, the traditional speculator's money-spinner, seldom commended itself to assessors (the pat on the back accorded to Portsmouth's unloved Tricorn Centre was surely an aberration), but by 1969, when the new central area of Blackburn received an Award, the lessons of several such spectacular failures, both aesthetic and commercial (the two were not unrelated), had begun to be learnt. Advantage is taken of the sloping ground to tuck servicing vehicles away out of sight, while cars are parked on top. Small courtyards with seats, flowers and fountains belie the size of the project and the whole is faced with a white tile which ten years later looks impeccable and sums up the miraculous 'Operation Eyesore' transformation of this beautifully situated but previously smoke-blackened mill town.

As for pastiche, to come to it finally, we no longer have to apologise for it. Horses for courses. To complete the enclosure of a Georgian Square in Bath it was no doubt the right answer (H 1975); for a NatWest bank on a corner site in Victorian Dartmouth (C 1980) it was no doubt a wrong one, even though correctly slate-hung, because it tends to devaluate the real thing and make life more monotonous all round. On the other hand the environmental gain

Before　　　　　　　　　　*After*

Jack Straw's Castle, Hampstead, London

St Michael's Arch, Abbey Green, Bath

National Westminster Bank, Dartmouth

61

through the replacement of a bad building on a conspicuous corner is un-questionable. The same goes for Jack Straw's castellated Castle (C 1964), the well-known Hampstead pub, a really nasty building gloriously transmogrified. The slightly embarrassed tone in which the Trust reported this naughty Commendation would have been unthinkable today. We even forgive the more arbitrary Gothicizing of a dull Victorian pair of houses in riverside Isleworth because, pale pink behind magnolias, it is such an obvious improvement, par-ticularly since next door the parish church, all but the tower of which was gutted by fire in 1943, has been brilliantly rebuilt (C 1973). The brick walls of the Georgian nave, furnished with the thick transoms that characterise the 1960s, now enclose a paved garden and pool which link the eroded medieval tower (under which one enters) with the new, square, red brick church. Delightful glimpses are to be had through slit windows, not least looking back to the tower, and hoisted (regrettably) up to the gallery are the marble Georgian tombs of a blind schoolteacher and of the man who endowed the old nave. This addition to the impeccable little waterfront is more than knitting: it is the transcending of constraints and the imaginative exploitation of limitations that are the essence of architecture.

*All Saints Church, Isleworth,
London*

Byker, Newcastle upon Tyne (page 70)

Living places

Three-quarters of our towns consist of living places and even those who go out to work spend three-quarters of their lives in them. But housing by its nature cannot compete with other kinds of building for glamour or originality and the two factors by which it mainly has to be judged in the real world, cost and convenience, are not those by which assessors are able to make these awards. So their judgments, and this section, cannot possibly measure up to the importance or complexity of the subject. The environmental quality of housing, by which they had to judged, is not most people's first criterion in choosing a dwellingplace. Nevertheless, this criterion has for a century and a half been so scandalously neglected that concentration on it can do nothing but good — indeed has done good, to judge by the enormous improvement in recent years.

There have been, as we saw earlier, three distinct phases in the postwar housing effort. The first, after some unrewarding experiments in small scale prefabrication, used conventional methods and reached its apogee in the 'mixed development' of the mid-fifties. The second, which we associate with the sixties, was the age of exploding demand and of high-rise system-building. Third, in the seventies, came the reaction to high-density low-rise and back to traditional materials. Assessors were not social analysts and had to search for the best of their respective kinds. It was fortunate that the scheme was not set up too late to honour the achievement of three outstanding architects in the fifties. Tayler & Green in a remote corner of Norfolk, starting as early as 1947, in the days when semi-detached houses were taken for granted in such areas, were able to persuade the Loddon Rural District Council to build long terraces

Housing for Loddon Rural District Council (left); A Span Development at Rayners Road, Wandsworth, London

of wide-fronted cottages charmingly detailed in the 'Festival' style and eminently suited to their exposed sites (A 1959). Eric Lyons, for Span Developments, starting in 1955 in the much cosier environment of south London, did a similar conversion job on the professional class in a series stretching over twenty years of small terraced groups which have been much imitated but never bettered. The sylvan beauty of the chosen sites, the superb quality of their new landscaping and the creation of owners' syndicates to manage them were the decisive factors. At the other end of the density scale, the third success story of the fifties was Westminster's Churchill Gardens on the banks of the Thames, won in competition in 1947 by two newly-qualified architects called Powell & Moya (A 1961). Unvandalized and well maintained (though regrettably infested with parked vehicles), this elegant central city housing proved to later gloomcasters that high-density flats do not have to be unloved.

As these proliferated through the sixties, assessors did their best to discriminate. Just east of Regent's Park there is an easily accessible live history book of the changing inner London housing fashions of this century, mostly the work of the old borough of St. Pancras. Of the four instalments, the two most

Winstanley Estate, Wandsworth, London

Churchill Gardens, Pimlico, London (top); Munster Square, Camden, London (photographed before the fencing-off of the ground floor)

67

attractive are the Crown Commissioners' graceful and symmetrical neo-Georgian Windsor House of 1930 and the Munster Square project of 1960 (A 1961), the latter an elegantly designed grey-and-white 'mixed development' of four-storey maisonettes and slim 18-storey towers in the prevailing LCC manner of the period. The open spaces are perfectly scaled for London and beautifully planted and maintained, and perhaps the only initial design fault is the squalid material used for the flat roofs on to which the tower dwellers have to look down. But no amount of municipal care can prevent the blight and alienation of the seventies from having infected the estate. As is usual the bases of the towers are the worst affected, and chain-link fencing, always a bad sign, has had to be inserted to protect ground-floor living-rooms from attack. A hundred yards to the west, beyond the class barrier of Albany Street, are Nash's superb and spotless Regent's Park terraces; but his architecture is no better.

And, of course, the GLC's great Pepys estate on the site of the naval dockyard west of Greenwich, which included the splendid rehabilitation of the 18th century terraces and warehouses, was irresistible (C 1970). Here the maisonettes, using the ingenious but unpopular 'scissors' section, went up to eight storeys and the towers to twenty-four. Aesthetically, and compared with the mass-housing going on all over the world at the time, this is an impeccable scheme. Grandly in scale with the wide and windy river, handsomely land-scaped, it has been at the same time carefully and intimately related with its Georgian setting, and the use of warm red brick for all except the widely spaced towers has to to a great extent protected it from the onslaughts of man and nature (though the underground garages have been vandalised as usual). But it *Pepys Estate, Lewisham, London* has suffered from the national dislike of gallery-access and pedestrian bridges,

and was one of the first great projects to prove that impressive architecture does not in itself make people happy. The system-built Winstanley estate (A 1967) near Clapham Junction, more human in scale, more snugly situated, proves the point. Now that the trees have grown we can see that thoughtful landscaping, soft and hard, can completely redeem high-density (by London standards) inner-city housing. Since it had to be built, this was the way to do it. Even in this pretty rough area it is a civilised environment. The same was hoped of the Glasgow equivalent. 'Careful thought,' wrote the assessor on the great Hutchesontown/Gorbals project (C 1966), 'for landscaping has evidently inspired the community to respect and to appreciate the nature of their new environment.' Alas, he spoke too soon.

This was by no means all that went on in the sixties. All over the country, notably in the new towns, decent low-rise housing, which was all anybody wanted, went up in quantity, while in inner areas of London, where this would obviously have been a solecism, terraced maisonettes were used to conserve the Victorian scale. Among the best are the GLC's elegant white terraces of old people's flats overlooking the Regent's Canal at Little Venice (C 1967), which introduce into this high-class white stucco environment a social and aesthetic admixture which does it nothing but good.

As the decade wore on the reaction against system-building and high-rise building in London gathered pace. But the undiminished demand now led to the overcrowding of small sites with Chinese-puzzle low-rise schemes, many built on top of communal garages and all in the newly-fashionable dark brick, which turned out equally unpopular and vulnerable to vandalism. Reporton Road in Hammersmith, given an Award in 1970, is a modest example of this

Warwick Estate, Little Venice, London

Head Street, Pershore,
Worcestershire (left); Low Fellside,
Kendal, Cumbria

misplaced ingenuity. For a brief period even Harlow New Town, generally so prodigal with space, turned over a new leaf. A competition for new ideas in housing won by a young architect in 1960 led to the building of Bishopsfield, a hard concrete-decked 'Casbah' which was immensely admired at the time and widely influential. It seems a stranger now, its blank-walled pedestrian slits and bleak communal square a misinterpretation of the Home Counties' life-style.

By the mid-seventies the lessons had been learnt and there were signs all over the country, not least in the North, that the pendulum had settled into a happy mean. The Northern Ireland Housing Executive set up by Roy Bradford in 1971 and now the largest housing authority in the UK, was by the mid-seventies well into its stride. In a reaction against out-of-town "estates" it took pains to interlock its very sensible vernacular terraces with their neighbours, as in the excellent cottages so neatly inserted into the heart of the attractive fishing village of Glenarm in Co Antrim (C 1980). In Newcastle the great Byker scheme was beginning to unfold (A 1979). Its slow pace was due to the deliberate decision to rehouse this old inner-city community on site and to the high degree of citizen participation this involved. One decision was not open to discussion — to shelter the whole slope from the north (and from a projected motorway that was never built) by a curving, rising and falling wall of small flats, smooth to the north but encrusted on its sunny side with little wooden balconies, pergolas and flights of steps. This produced a micro-climate that enabled the designer to fill every spare yard of low-rise housing in the lee of the wall with vegetation and so contrive an environment never before imagined on this bleak coast. The eccentric, rather flimsy, quite un-Novocastrian detailing can be taken as a nice change after the brutalist years. Over the same period,

Lyde End, Bledlow,
Buckinghamshire (left);
Aberdeen Park, Islington, London

first in Kendal and later in Perth, in outworn areas close to their town centres, new white harled housing was contrived that fitted into its environment like the last piece of a jigsaw puzzle. In Kendal (H 1975) this was partly due to the picturesque exploitation of a steep slope and the re-use of old steps and alleys; in Perth (A 1980) to delightful vernacular architecture and the rebuilding of the old walls, railings, and slipway along the prettily wooded bend of the Tay.

Up and down the country, just as a virtual moratorium has been imposed on it, public housing is now so good that it is as invidious for me to choose as it must have been for assessors. Only three neatly detailed, generously planted, unaffected groups of brick housing can here be mentioned as a minute sample: one group of curved terraces in the North, where Washington New Town in County Durham has done excellent work (Albany VII Phase A 1979); one in the Midlands, where architects by now expert in such work, using first a lusciously warm red brick and later a cooler pinker one, have for many years charmingly exploited odd corners in the handsome Georgian-fronted town of Pershore (H 1975); and one in London. Hard to find in the green oasis of Aberdeen Park in Islington (A 1981) is a brown brick group of houses by the same architects which seem to embody all the lessons that have been learnt in the last thirty years. To say that the scheme converts two tall Victorian villas and uses their back gardens for new housing and a pedestrian short-cut conveys nothing of its quality. The new terraces, varying in height between four storeys and one, enclose their green heart as though they had always been there. Strictly in conformity with Government cost limits and density requirements, they give the opposite impression — of timelessness, classlessness; or urban living at its most life-enhancing.

Having inevitably concentrated on the public sector, it seems only right to end with examples of three other kinds of housing, all of outstanding quality. Clump Field (A 1972), a horseshoe of small flats tucked into a natural amphitheatre on the south slope of the beautifully wooded eastern suburbs of Ipswich, is a model Housing Association project and an early example of the brown-brick, stained-wood style that was to spread so rapidly in the last years of the decade. The holiday village on the slate quay at Portmadoc (A 1978) is an equally tight cluster, which it can be, needing no gardens, and needs to be on this exposed, magnificent site. The contrast with romantic, richly-wooded Portmeirion across the water is intriguing, and not damaging to the younger enterprise, though it inevitably seems flimsy over against the massive harbour walls and warehouses of Madocks's port. In total and exhilarating contrast is a little jewel in the South. No photograph can do justice to this modest group of cottages for a private landowner in the hamlet of Bledlow just below the Chiltern escarpment (A 1978). It rises quite dramatically, like a Burgundian fortified farm, above a ravine watered by a little brook. On the gravelled courtyard side the grouping is masterly, yet with never a hint of sentimentality. Every brick, one feels, has been lovingly laid. Yet it could date from no period but our own. How sad that the trees which provided its backdrop have gone.

Finally, a single private house in the heart of historic Hampstead (A 1979), a Cheshire Cat of a house, so transparent that it is easy on a summer's day not to spot it, in its nest of willows, where it takes advantage of the shade of a tall block of Edwardian flats to the south-west. When you do, you will be astonished at its lightness and grace: even the roof, remarkably for England, has been conjured away.

49a Downshire Hill, Camden, London

Building for Education

In the eyes of the world the most interesting building going on in Britain in the fifties was the prefabricated schools programme. But it did not occur to the county architects concerned, whether in Herts, Notts or Sussex, to put in for Civic Trust awards. Scattered about in the new housing estates in the urban fringes, the new schools presumably seemed to have no great environmental significance. Others, however, felt differently, and the sixties saw a number of awards and commendations going to new schools of all kinds and sizes. Typical of the period are two in London for backward children, the first situated in a district of magnificent 18th century oaks at Southgate in north London (A 1967), with a rather elementary and under-designed classroom block redeemed by an elegant *Look-no-hands* assembly-hall roof. A lot of white-painted woodwork (which would nowadays be plastic) has set the local authority a maintenance problem which it has confronted with commendable persistence. Consequently, the building still looks happy. The second looks across a green slope to the charming toy church of Belvue, a few yards north of the roaring Western Avenue in Ealing (A 1967). This sensitively designed little yellow-stock brick building is, by contrast, a disgrace. Its shingled-roofed assembly hall is now walled off by a 20ft high chain-linked fence, its paintwork is peeling, its corrugated perspex roofing full of holes, and its perimeter infested with rotting huts and a hideous garage built of asbestos imitating stonework: a training-establishment for vandals.

Of course it isn't easy to control the environment of schools. Bikes and dustbins accumulate in odd corners, tarmac has to be patched, teachers Sellotape papers to windows as blithely as supermarkets, children do what damage they can. The long, low, fully glazed Halifax School (C 1972) on a hill above Ipswich is a case in point. Designed on a precast concrete grid system devised by the architects, to an open plan desired by an enlightened head-master, its Miesian elegance has been further compromised by a recent white repaint of its glazing-bars which is enough to ruin its proportions. Church schools are on the whole more disciplined. Thus the Rosary School on a conspicuous crest in the happy-go-lucky mill town of Stroud (A 1968) still looks very handsome, its previously white asbestos siding having turned to a silver grey that gives a passable imitation of weathered cedar.

In dramatic contrast to all these cool buildings of the sixties is Fort Hill School (A 1980) on high ground hard to find in the vast stretches of windy suburbia that now engulf Basingstoke. Generously spread out, wholly built of warm red brick and warm red pantiles, with much use of soldier courses, with lots of little stained wooden windows, it even has ceramic spur ridge-tiles at the foot of its roof-hips to underline its Japanese affiliations. Elegant planting and brick paving complete the picture, and it will be fascinating to see how time and taste will treat it.

If the new schools were, by and large, unpretentious, stripped-down buildings, designed (in the public sector) down to firm cost and size limits imposed by Ministry architects who knew what they were talking about, the 22 new universities built in Britain over the same period had been won in fierce competition by proud cities and regions and were seen as representative of their prestige. So they chose masterful architects likely to get their way with a University Grants Committee which lacked the Ministry's practical experience,

University of York, Langwith and Derwent Colleges (top); The Great Hall, Bell Tower and Concourse, University of Wales, Aberystwyth (page 81)

filling any financial gaps by local fund-raising. They were right to do so, for their building programmes were highly diversified and specialised and in some ways more complex than those of the New Towns, which were far more strongly staffed. Most of the new universities were built on beautiful rural sites out of sight, and out of mind, of their parent towns, and were towns, of a sort themselves. They were the most exciting architectural opportunities of their age.

Consequently, they were immensely award-worthy. But they presented the problem of all stretched-out programmes: when, and to what, to give the prize. To the model? To the first completed phase? To an individual building? Obviously they would never be 'finished,' and for many years they would be building sites, with immature landscaping. Assessors solved the problem in different ways. Sussex, first out of the ground, went unrecognised until 1969, when Spence's beehive-like centre-piece, the University Meeting House (and interdenominational chapel) received a deserved Award. The assessor did not claim this as a recognition of the success of the whole, but we may take it as such, for Sussex sits well in its downland valley, nicely diversified and not too rigidly bound to the aesthetic of its original designer.

In the case of York, Lancaster and East Anglia, Awards went to the entire university as it stood in 1968 and 1969, and this seems right, because all three in their dramatically different ways were total concepts, not loose master plans tolerant of a variety of individual contributions. York's philosophy was that a university had no higher claim than a school to one-off works of Architecture, and that only system-building (CLASP borrowed from Nottinghamshire) could hit the time and cost targets. The aesthetic drawbacks, the drab finishes and the crude proportions that result from the assembly of a limited number of large components, were to be mitigated by an impressive slung-roofed assembly hall, by various skyline features and above all by a large and romantically landscaped artificial lake, perhaps the best demonstration in England of what water and trees can do for architecture. East Anglia (A 1969), concrete too, is otherwise in total contrast. Where York's stand about an informal relationship, these masses are bound together in a single overpowering sculptural form, superbly related to the gentle willow-filled valley it overlooks. The nicest things about East Anglia is the domestically-scaled group of fully-glazed residential ziggurats, the nastiest the concrete academic jungle at its heart, confusing on account of the

University of Lancaster

45-degree configuration and the unpopular vertical segregation of vehicles from pedestrians. The constriction and exposure of the elevated walkways, once committed to which there is no escaping the unwelcome don heading towards one, have caused much muddy diversion on to the deliberately hazardous and circuitous ground below. Recent additions (as in the cities) have brought life back on to the ground wherever possible. As to the pervasive concrete itself, the failure to be aware of what Berenson called 'tactile values' is that of a whole generation. Lancaster (A 1968) is different again. Its designers saw it as a snug hill-town, with a village street and a series of Oxbridge-sized, warm brick courts shielding the resident from the rainy west winds. Its architecture is secondary to its planning, indeed allows itself to be quite ordinary, as urban design can afford to be if the spaces it encloses are nicely scaled. Its quadrangular principle of growth enables it to look complete at all stages.

The University of Stirling, the first new foundation in Scotland since Edinburgh in 1583, was recognised (A 1968) at the stage of its first major teaching building. This, the Pathfoot, is a long layered building, whose considerable floor-space is belied by the wooded slope into which it nestles on gently rising levels with strong horizontal emphasis, the whole reflected in the dark loch below. Standing apart from the central complex across the water and from taller residences nearby, this graceful building seems to have stood the test of time both functionally and visually, and remains one of Scotland's best buildings of the sixties.

Less romantically but more dramatically sited is the Great Hall, Bell Tower and Concourse for the University of Wales at Aberystwyth (A 1971). High on a windswept sunset-facing slope, it commands not only the whole town in its horseshoe of hills but the whole of the Irish Sea — a true acropolis, if you have the physique to enjoy it, and a place that (at the opposite pole from Oxbridge) almost enforces spacious thoughts — or windy generalisation! The slope is well used to tuck away parking under the great podium, the campanile is admirably simple and well-scaled and only the Hall itself disappoints: top ends of lecture halls project without drama, the main entrance is suppressed, and the whole fails to express its centrality. The assessor hoped the buildings' finishes would stand up to the weather; in fact, after a decade the granite-faced slabs have done so impeccably.

While these stars shone in their spacious landscapes, the old red-brick colleges, translated into universities or polytechnics, set about polishing up their images. This they badly needed to do, after a postwar decade described in the *Architectural Review* of October 1975 as 'unspeakably dim and dreary.' Lanchester College of Technology, the Bauhaus of the then prosperous British motor industry, was rehoused in the heart of ruined Coventry right alongside the new Cathedral. Like so much English architecture through the ages, this is a cut-price and scaled-down version of a foreign exemplar, in this case appropriately Mies van der Rohe's Crown Hall (the design school) in the Illinois Institute of Technology. As foil and modest mirror to the red sandstone neo-neo-Gothic cathedral it was an excellent solution, reflecting its use as well (A 1966). It has worn well, too, but its dignity has been sadly impaired by a crude and vulgar illuminated sign across its front.

Another excellent morale-booster was a new assembly hall-cum-theatre. In the North-East two not dissimilar buildings, both highly sculptural, do this most effectively for the red-brick universities of Hull (C 1969) and Newcastle

Lanchester College of Technology, Coventry (top left) The Gulbenkian Centre. University of Hull (top right) (page 83); The Theatre, University of Newcastle upon Tyne (bottom left); (page 83); Darwin Building, Royal College of Art, London (page 83)

81

(A 1972). Both were only a small, but distinguished, fraction of expansion programmes co-ordinated and largely executed by the very best of our architects. Hull's Gulbenkian Centre, now hemmed in by larger buildings, makes little impact, but Newcastle's University Theatre stands up boldly across the motorway from the Civic Centre. This frontage was slotted to receive a high-level bridge that has not been built, but the architect anticipated such a possibility and the building looks if anything better without it, both without and within. The use of the same red-brown brick for this and Sheppard and Robson's excellent adjacent buildings gives the post-war campus unity as well as distinction. In London, of course, such additions had no campus to slot into: they had to take their place as street architecture and solve the problems touched on in an earlier section. Such was the Royal College of Art's workshop block in Kensington Gore (A 1964), 'fashionably sombre to the point of melancholy, thought the assessor: 'one imagines apprehensively how it might affect a failed student on a damp, grey February day.' Wisely lowered a couple of storeys by the Royal Fine Art Commission to the approximate height of Norman Shaw's Albert Hall Mansions, the nicest thing about the building is its shade-dappled courtyard, which appropriates to itself the huge rotundity of the Albert Hall. But the Albert Hall upstaged it in terms of colour in 1970 when it turned from black to red and cream (C 1973). The new building replaced some Regency houses and a decade later would not have been allowed.

But, of course, the great exponents of urban infill were the old sisters, Oxford and Cambridge. They deserve a section to themselves.

Oxford and Cambridge

Volumes have been written about the failure of postwar planning in these cities and the successes of postwar architecture. This note, confined to the fraction of new building honoured by the Civic Trust, should first record that when the awards were set up in 1957 the modern movement had yet to show its face in either university. Sir Giles Scott, Sir Hubert Worthington and Sir Herbert Baker were the leading lights of the inter-war period, and Cotswold stone with Clipsham dressings (for Oxford) or two-inch grey or brown handmade bricks with Portland dressings (for Cambridge) were still the correct wear. Nothing approaching the size of Scott's two libraries had been possible since the war, and nobody dreamt of whole new Colleges. It had been a very dull decade.

St. John's, Oxford, advised by a courageous Bursar, seems to have been the first, in the late fifties, to admit modern architecture on to the premises to fill a gap in a minor quad away from the main axis (A 1960). It was brave, even quix-otic, of the architect to introduce two novelties at once — Portland Stone and hexagonal planning — the latter, complete with faintly Byzantine lanterns, a rather restless arrival in the traditionally rectilinear scene. But the modest scale of the building and the new paving made it acceptable and it has worn well. It was followed by a small masterpiece. Even more obscurely situated in the inner-most recesses of Brasenose this first Oxbridge essay by two young architects instead of creating a new space abolished an old one, but did it with such assurance and ingenuity that Powell & Moya became the darlings of the dons in both universities (A 1963). From now on, in accordance with precedent, half a dozen names recur indiscriminately in both universities, and it seems sensible

St John's College, Oxford (top); Corpus Christi College, Magpie Lane, Oxford (page 85)

St Anne's College, Oxford

Extension for Christ Church College from Blue Boar Lane, Oxford

to skip to and fro with them. They were well chosen. Philip Dowson of Arup Associates was another. An East Anglian, his first assignment was on the leafy western side of Cambridge — a graduate hostel in the vast garden of an Edwardian house, among superb trees (A 1965). This spare, vertebrate, graceful building is an early example of an obsession with the separation of frame from panels which characterised the architect's work in that decade. A year later Somerville College, Oxford, was commended for a similar design, slung over a row of shops in a much more commonplace environment. An Award that year (1966) went to two Cambridge architects for an Oxford building — the new Law Library in Manor Road. This is an expansive building faced with blond bricks appropriate in colour, with a touch of Frank Lloyd Wright in its long horizontals and of Alvar Aalto in its splendid steps — a rare exception to the English tendency to reduce a monumental idea down to residential scale. Unfortunately, its black anodised aluminium trim has turned a lurid shade of purple.

Another firm of Oxbridge regulars were already at work in both universities. In Cambridge, HKPA (in current abbreviation) were building the University Centre on the Cam (C 1968). Where the gently rising Oxford Library belies its size, this club building, squeezed into an inadequate site beside a modest pub, proclaims it by giving separate and rather crude expression to every element in its composition, even the bolts that hold the cast stone facing slabs. It conse-

quently feels all the more misplaced. Yet simultaneously in a cedar-shaded north Oxford garden the same architects produced the first of a curvaceous group of residential buildings, laid out head to tail like a train on a gentle bend with a gracefulness wholly appropriate to a women's college (A 1969). The bellows-camera window, later to become a tiresome cliché, here makes an early and innocuous appearance.

Meanwhile, Powell & Moya, now unexcelled knitters, dropped two more ingenious sets of rooms into the secluded heart of medieval Oxford. One, in Magpie Lane for Corpus (A 1969), has bold concrete-framed glass bays emerging from Cotswold rubble in deference to the old wall it replaced. This did not obviate the following graffiti on the slate panels conveniently provided at eye level: 'Remember Magpie Lane once beautiful now spoilt by Corpus vandalism,' countered by 'Why does Oriel have such extremely boring walls?' Fortunately, in Blue Boar Lane close by there was depth enough to tuck in behind a similar wall, beyond which loom up grand gloomy buttresses in roach-bed Portland, a more dramatic, more Oxonian effect than on the quad side, where the building displays a rather weak curve (C 1969). Larger still, though almost invisible from outside its purlieus, is the Cripps Building for St. John's Cambridge (A 1968), and this has space to breathe — a share of the meandering backwaters of the Cam and wide lawns along its rambling length. The walk along the undercroft

The Law Library, Oxford

of this great building is a lovely experience, with water and grass alternating among sun-dappled trees. Ancillary buildings, already much weathered, are sculptural and full of character, with a trough-like bridge giving escape to the outside world. The general effect of the building, which is elaborately trabeated, is perhaps rather fussy after the smooth domestic Gothic of the earlier courts. All three are significant late 20th century contributions to the two most important collections in Britain of six centuries of domestic and public architecture.

But many unpretentious buildings, away from the medieval core, have enriched the two cities. Two Cambridge examples by local architects are the delightful nurses' hostel on Trumpington Road (A 1978), perhaps rather Celtic in manner for East Anglia, and the little addition to the random bunch of small buildings that is Darwin College, 'placed like a book-end,' said the assessor, in Silver Street (C 1980). The pretty slatted balconies are a 1980 touch which may look better over time if they are painted. In Oxford I mention an early example, the malthouse conversion in Headington, commended in 1960, because it commemorates the excellent work on a modest scale done all over the city by the Surveyor to the University (not, by the way, himself an architect). This last leads naturally to another major Oxford achievement of the period, the refacing and cleaning of virtually the whole of the historic buildings of the university and its colleges through an appeal which raised £2.4m. Not everybody approved.

Darwin College, Cambridge

Cripps Building, St John's College, Cambridge

Christ Church Library (unlike its superbly done-up opposite number in Cambridge) lost its atmosphere of gloomy Roman decay and, ten years after the initial pale golden miracle, the colleges have settled into a brownish uniformity less evocative than the old peeling shadows. But the state of the Headington stone was such that it had to be done, and its legacy is a comforting sense of security.

Both universities have been the scene of more ingenious infill than any other English cities, giving the impression that every single institution within them has had a baby or two. The effect, particularly on the western fringes of Cambridge, is far from restful. That bland white-brick city, previously reddened by only a few late Victorian or Edwardian foundations, is now multi-coloured and over-designed, with few architects daring to be as ordinary as their predecessors. This, of course, was only to be expected in architects of sensibility looking out upon the work of their commercial contemporaries. In both universities Portland Stone, in Oxford hitherto scarcely used at all and in Cambridge only affordable for the grandest of showpieces, has been used for residential extensions and injects into the hitherto cosy scene a rather cool austerity, and lead appears a lot in new situations. This second Elizabethan period is likely to be seen, looking back, as a highly mannered and insecure period, in this respect unexpectedly echoing the first.

Chrysler-Cummins Factory, Darlington

Workplaces

It was the policy of the wartime Abercrombie plans for London to move industry, with its workers, out of the city, preferably to the new and expanded towns, and later on as a result of the office boom the same policy was applied to office buildings too and a special Bureau set up to push it along. Eventually, and not only in London, the consequent exodus of young workers and their families came to be regretted by everybody except them, but nobody could regret the architectural consequences. Industrialists were able to take their pick of magnificent and conspicuous greenfield sites on which it was worthwhile to employ prestigious architects. Two majestic examples from the late sixties are here illustrated: the Chrysler/Cummins engineering works on the edge of Darlington (A 1966) and the Horizon tobacco factory on the edge of Nottingham (A 1972). The twin factories on the eastern edge of Darlington, one shiny blue-black brick with slit windows and a huge brick drum-like tower (containing what?) the other in brown Cor-ten steel and brown glass, spread themselves American-style on the wide green plain. The first has a slightly sinister and secret character, the second is classically Miesian. Both are impeccably maintained and as the trees grow will continue to improve. The Nottingham factory reflects even more dramatically than the Darlington ones the futurist idealisation of Industry. But its repose is classical. It stands palatially on its impeccably maintained green slopes, a superbly confident composition. Recent minor alterations have been done with tact, though they could with advantage have included some more trees, particularly in the parking areas.

It would be wrong not to include with these monuments of industrial architecture one of the power stations of the same generation, the vastest constructions ever imposed on our countryside. Cockenzie, built partly on reclaimed land on the south shore of the Firth of Forth, has the benefit of an equally vast seascape as foreground or background, and exploits it (A 1971). With glazed turbine house and slim chimneys and, of course, having the sea, no cooling towers, it is a classic of its period, so that the windy walk between it and the sea, opened up for the first time to the public, is an exhilarating experience.

Industrial buildings as major monuments rising out of an American-style landscaped campus were a characteristic feature of the expansive sixties. But with the campaign to revive the inner city, the eighties are going to see a very different industrial image. Turn right into the last junction at the top end of Ladbroke Grove and you find yourself in the scruffy, nondescript region of miscellaneous workshops and warehouses that you can still find all over London, despite the efforts of earlier planners to clean them up. Then suddenly you come on a building such as you have never seen before — bold yet relaxed, colourful yet classically austere. Giant brick columns, striped in blue, red and yellow (the three colours of London brickwork) giant concrete bollards, floating white pediments under whose generous cantilevers huge lorries can shelter, glazed, timber-framed offices perched on a minor order of columns. This is nothing more than a cut-price row of lettable factories, except that it is also nothing less than one of the best buildings in London (A 1981). It has the stamp of that rarest thing in architecture — an original mind.

Office buildings, our other largest artefacts, now fall as a result of decentralization into two distinct categories, urban and rural. The urban category probably includes more bad or boring buildings than any other

Chrysler-Cummins Factory, Darlington (top); Offices of Northern Gas Board, Killingworth (page 95) (middle); The Horizon Factory for John Player Ltd, Nottingham

because, like housing in the 19th century, it became the playground of cynics and exploiters. Nevertheless good people *were* involved, even though they were a smaller minority in this field than elsewhere. The first out of the ground, the Crown Commissioners' long block facing Paddington Station (A 1961), was one of the best, and none the worse for being extremely profitable. Its masculine and unaffected architecture has worn extraordinarily well, not least due to the London stock bricks with which it is faced. Nearly twenty years later its architect was to go on to rescue Victoria Street by means of another equally long but very different pile of office buildings, through a gap in which he opened up a magical glimpse of Bentley's Byzantine cathedral and a new urban space (C 1979). The Elephant & Castle blocks (A 1964), now the headquarters of the DHSS, Corbusian in inspiration and the only convincing occupants of a sadly muddled and misused Comprehensive Development Area, have weathered as gloomily as concrete does in London and were said by a 1978 critic (who had obviously never met the ebullient architect) to convey a 'contemptuous conception of life's value.' In fact the polished granite at ground level holds the dark sculptural concrete above at a decent distance, and the group still has an individuality and expressiveness strong enough even to survive the ramshackle addition of what look like flyscreens, but are presumably cut-price *brises-soleil*, on its sunny sides. In contrast to these rough beasts are the twin occupants

90

(Commercial Union and P&O) of the site in Leadenhall Street they were able to turn into a New-York-type piazza through their collaboration (A 1970) — itself a rare example of two companies coming together for the public good. The taller tower is an elegantly Miesian glass box, still perhaps the best in London, but the piazza itself, exposed in wet weather and done on the cheap with excessive ups and downs for drainage, is a little disappointing, opening up, as they are apt to, bits of old buildings that were never meant to be seen. Far neater occupants of their respective townscapes, though on a far smaller scale, are two little glass buildings in the North. MEA House in Newcastle (C 1979) brilliantly (and at some cost in construction) exploits a misshapen site thrown up by large-scale road works and in the process, perhaps by accident, is delightfully jammed up against a Georgian terrace. The CEGB Regional office in Harrogate (C 1980) is smooth-skinned reflective architecture at its happiest, and it has some pretty planting to reflect. It is hard to imagine a building more uncharacteristic of that substantial and respectable town.

Eastbourne Terrace, Paddington, London (left); Alexander Fleming House, Elephant and Castle, London

An altogether grander example of reflective glass architecture is the Clydesdale Bank's new building in the heart of mid-Victorian Glasgow (C 1981).

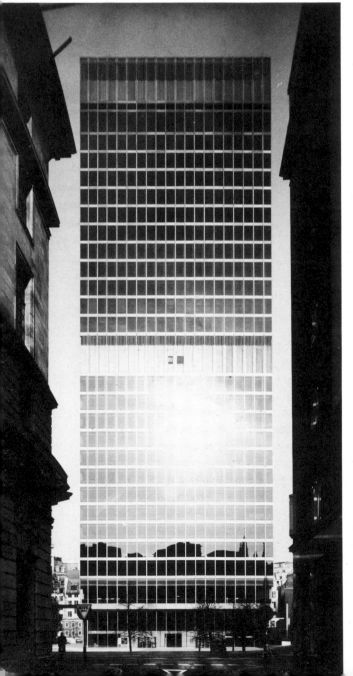

Once to have been a tower block, this is the happy ending of a long story of consultation and argument. Dark red granite and dark tinted glass gives the building a strong surface affinity with its rather sombre neighbours, amid which the little church tower of St. George's seems almost light-hearted. Base storey, main order, cornice, roof lines and window proportions tie in with neighbours, and its air of quality and even opulence places the building firmly in the tradition of Glasgow's commercial palaces.

The earliest of our 'rural' examples is appropriately the British offshoot of an international concern from a country which has been building this way for a long time. The Heinz building at Hayes (A 1967) managed to obtain for itself an almost Arcadian setting (the park of a demolished country house) tucked away out of sight of the nightmare region of inter-war muddle that stretches out beyond Ealing as far as Uxbridge. It is a monumentally-proportioned example of the mainstream International Style, faultlessly detailed and in geometrical contrast, as any classical villa should be, with the 'natural' landscape, above which it floats on stubby *pilotis*. But it needs to be white, as originally photographed. Grey now, and stained along its parapet here and there, its sparkle has gone, and it fails to assert, as an elegant country house should, its superiority over the splendidly tall garden walls above which it rises. The offices and research station for the Northern Gas Board at Killingworth on the windy plateau north of Newcastle (C 1968) is, admittedly, in a New Town, but only a baby one initiated by the County Council, and its spacious setting by a lake is certainly not urban. It is a highly 'conceptual' group of buildings, the sculptural research block in effective contrast with the elegant glass office, and the Minoan motif works superbly.

The culmination of a remarkable story of enlightened patronage by the rival purveyors of gas and electricity is the CEGB regional headquarters at Bedminster Down (A 1980), embedded into the crest of a lightly suburbanized ridge on the south-west fringes of Bristol, which commands a superb view to the Clifton Gorge and the towers and spires of the city. In plan this is a symmetrical group of square courts and pavilions on a 'tartan' grid, with very low-pitched, very deep-eaved, slate roofs gently rising to two pyramidal skylights. It is approached and then threaded by a wide, smooth-tiled, central pathway whose street-like character is reinforced by gentle slopes up and down and which emerges eventually on to the great northward panorama. This runs not along the axis of symmetry but, in a gesture of deliberate informality, at right angles to it. Off it are two levels of carpeted office spaces, lit from inner courts as well as from generous outward-facing stained wood windows. Out of sight below is a mass of plant and parking, enfolded in the smooth green curves of the remodelled landscape. The architects' three objectives — a gentle impact on the landscape, a humane and relaxed working environment and a minimal use of energy — are triumphantly achieved in what is unquestionably a masterpiece of our age. Not far away, not attempting to fly so high, and not in the open country but tucked away on the banks of the Avon upstream from the centre of Bath is the Herman Miller furniture factory (C 1978). This long biscuit-coloured glass-fibre shed does not pretend to be more than that. Its sliding panels are adjustable *ad lib* to suit internal rearrangement and it typifies the cool approach of its architects (and their addiction at that time to the rounded-off right angle).

The Heinz Building, Hayes, London (top); Commercial Union Offices, City of London (far left); MEA House, Newcastle upon Tyne (right top); Clydesdale Bank, Glasgow (right middle); CEGB Regional Offices, Harrogate

Public Buildings

Whereas our housing is incomparably better than a century ago, it would be absurd to expect our public and institutional buildings to emulate either the rhetoric or the craftsmanship of the Victorians. 'The ratepayers would not stand for it.' Victorian and Edwardian public architecture celebrated national wealth, civic competitiveness and bourgeois vanity, not unmixed with unacknowledged guilt: the poor were 'always with us,' but could at least be elevated by noble architecture. Local politicians now know that, second to a decent home, voters will support an exciting Leisure Centre or a convenient shopping complex, but not a Mayoral Suite. So our public buildings do not attempt the centrality or the monumentality of their forbears: they leave that to the old Town Hall, to which many of them are correctly ancillary.

Newcastle Civic Centre (A 1969) is, of course, an exception. Designed in 1951, it is stylistically the last of the vaguely Scandinavian town halls of between-the-wars. But there is a great advance from, say, Norwich. Of attenuated Swedish neo-classic there is no vestige: symmetry is out. The sea-horses atop the carillon tower may be the kind of thing nobody would have done ten years later; the elements of the building are taken apart and assembled in the loose-jointed manner of the fifties and there is a pleasant atmosphere of accessibility, sadly compromised by the seventies' siege mentality and shortage of staff. Of course it should have been faced with the tawny stone of Grey Street, but the white Portland makes a marvellous background for the coal-black tower (long may it remain so) of St. Thomas' Church.

The rebuilt heart of Coventry is another period piece, its main axis and mildly bricky character fully established before the Awards came into existence. By the time the City Arcade was submitted (A 1963) Ling had succeeded Gibson as City Architect and post-war red-brick, already considered dated, was replaced by mainstream black brick and steel, smarter but more anonymous, the natural product of a much larger office. But Coventry centre on a Saturday morning is a good place to be and despite being the daddy of them all, shows only one sign of obsolescence — the hike from your rooftop car park past the squalid backs of shops, like a ballroom you can only reach through the back door and the scullery. Once you reach it the four arms of the cross, each closed by a vertical landmark, meet with a satisfying sense of centrality. It is still a lot better than most of the commercial developers were later able to manage.

Meanwhile the new breed of accessible, unpompous Civic Centres was getting into its stride, first off the mark, surprisingly, in the proud old ship-building port of Sunderland. Here the Council decided not to shoe-horn it into the shabby grid of central shopping streets but to exploit wasteland it owned on adjacent high ground. The result is a brilliant essay in steps, ramps and low enclosed courts (A 1972). It has been criticized for crowning its hill with no land-mark but a louvred ventilator and, watching mothers with prams negotiating the criss-cross ramps as though on the summit cone of Snowdon, one could blame it for this too. But on a fine day it is hard to do so. The building sparkles as though new in its shining brown tile facing and is linked by an elegant footbridge to one of the most pleasurable and adventurous little parks in England. In contrast to this green and airy campus, Wolverhampton, seven years later (A 1979), has built in the very heart of the old hill-town. This is a modestly and sensitively-scaled brown brick building, its only affectation the

The City Arcade, Coventry

Newcastle upon Tyne Civic Centre (top); The Crown Court, Manchester (bottom left); Sunderland Civic Centre

97

glacis base first introduced into England by Saarinen in his American Embassy. On the south it defines a new central square, properly dominated, as is the whole town centre, by the grand 15th century parish church on the crest of the slope. Wide steps ascend under the building on to this nicely-scaled civic space, with Wheeler's pleasant figure of the lady who gave the land for the church as its frontispiece. Below, the new building modestly allows the 1870 Town Hall to lord it as of old. Wolverhampton is no upstart town and its Civic Centre confirms this by its very absence of ostentation. Those who speak of the arrogance of architects should visit it.

Manchester is a very different sort of place both historically and geographically, with a metropolitan scale and a tradition of arrogance. The new Crown Courts (A 1972) here too provided the opportunity for the creation of a new square, the formality of which is unfortunately compromised to the north by Albert Bridge House, a commercial development orientated without any regard to the grain of the city centre. The Courts themselves are strictly symmetrical and have a continental grandeur of scale. Faced in glazed white tile, which unlike white mosaic has so far remained pristine, they demonstrate how these two qualities, size and symmetry, without a vestige of 'ornament' or rhetoric, can convey classical grandeur in unmistakable terms.

By the middle sixties increasing Government patronage and the theatrical renaissance led to the building, while the going was good, of new civic or university theatres, of which Sheffield's and Nottingham's were the most distinguished architecturally. But whereas Sheffield's spacious, hexagonally planned Crucible (A 1972) cannot do much for an architecturally disorderly site, Nottingham's Playhouse (A 1966) has transformed its surroundings without dominating them. It is tucked away rather unexpectedly in a quiet, modest Victorian square, to which it contributes an appropriate black-and-white sparkle impervious to the passage of time. Nowadays its brick podium would

Wolverhampton Civic Centre

Nottingham Playhouse in 1966

Swimming Pool, Richmond,
North Yorkshire (A 1978)

have been red to conform with fashion and complement the neighbours. It is incidentally even more effective after dark, as a theatre should be. More riskily, a London contemporary, the Royal College of Physicians (A 1967) invades the heart of Nash's Regent Park stage-set, one of a series of such challenges its architect was to meet head-on. It now seems extraordinary that this graceful *pavilion* (its elegance achieved, as so often, at some cost in structural logic) should have excited so much controversy. Grimier now, with moss growing until recently in the joints of its fascinating twisted brick lecture hall, it now seems a modest and subtly understated building. The superb interior space demonstrates what an uplift white walls can give to mediocre presidential portraits. If one misses the exterior sparkle here, what is one to say of the Queen Elizabeth Hall and Hayward Gallery on the South Bank (A 1970) described by its assessor as 'a most stimulating environment?' He did add that 'all that remains is for hotels and shops to be built nearby to attract the people needed to bring the place alive at all times'.) It is now itself the frequent subject of remedial exercises and experiments, and the gallery interior has to be reconstructed at vast expense for every Arts Council exhibition. In the same year a maintenance depot for British Rail (A 1970) neatly slotted into the highway

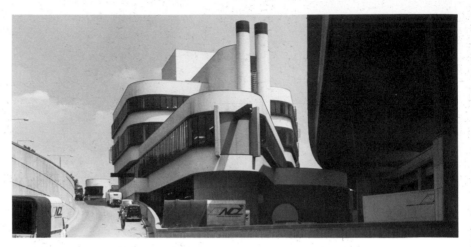

*Paddington Maintenance Depot,
London*

*Queen Elizabeth Hall and
Hayward Gallery on the South
Bank, London*

*Opposite page
The Royal College of
Physicians overlooking
Regent's Park, London (top);
Metro Travel Interchange,
Bradford (A 1979)*

spaghetti in the shadow of Westway, consciously derivative and curvaceous in
the manner of 1925 Eric Mendelsohn, seemed to have swopped clothes with
the Hayward, which has all the look of a maintenance depot. But it too looked
better pristine and is now scarcely noticed.

My last public building is the Liverpool terminal of the B&I ferry to Dun
Laoghaire, seen in 1970 as the centrepiece of the revival of this stretch of the
decayed waterfront, and fairly described by its 1972 assessor as 'all sweetness
and grace'. The irony was not then perceptible. Much has happened since. The
high enclosed gangway does not fit the new ships, and since there was no flexibility for this predictable contingency an appalling 'temporary' steel contraption
has replaced it, with flights of steps that make no allowance for the disabled.
Secondly, the troubles in Ireland have changed the role of this optimistic ex-
trovert building: it is now on the defensive, its careful landscaping destroyed by
chain-link and barbed wire. Metal finishes have suffered from the salty air,
lighting from the vibration of ships' engines moored alongside, then replaced
by a non-architect-designed and totally unsympathetic fluorescent system. A
sad story, made the sadder by the owners' failure to take qualified advice on
essential modifications.

Improvement

Searching for such needles of hope in the haystacks of West Yorkshire or Merseyside or the formless fringes of London was often a dispiriting business. Could the vast mass ever be redeemed? Not, obviously, by large organisations, public or private, however enlightened. Still less by small ones, even as inspired as the Landmark Trust, operating nationally. It could only ever be done on the spot, by the imaginations and efforts of countless individuals, banded together or alone. To these EAHY 1975 was an invaluable stimulus, or recognition. It was the outward and visible sign of what is now, unquestionably, a Movement.

Every individual who, caring for his house, enters into its spirit without thinking he has to better it, is a contributor. Such was Gerald Ogilvie-Laing, who took over a floorless, nearly roofless little castle in remotest Wester Ross (A 1971), uninhabited since 1918, removed later accretions, restored the 1594 building, bar three little dormers to light his roofspace: 'aesthetics,' reported the assessor, 'took precedence over practicality.' Such were the Thomas brothers of Outwood Common in Surrey, who devoted twenty years to the piece by piece renewal of a great 17th century post mill (C 1980). In the cities, such people often take the lead in forming a housing association to do up a whole terrace, like the residents of 28-62 Barnsbury Street in Islington (A 1973), which was nearly derelict and scheduled for demolition but now, with the aid of local authority grants, back in its early 19th century dignity in every detail. On an even grander scale, the residents of the Woodlands area (A 1979) in the heart of Glasgow took on half a square mile of four-storey red sandstone tenements and with strong support from the local authority did it all up and cleaned it and reorganised and repaired its surroundings. A welcome side-effect is that the whole operation has brought a number of ethnic minorities into a friendly working relationship. Sometimes a brave act of faith was needed, as with Robert Owen's barrack-like tenements at New Lanark (A 1971), in their wooded gorge, so significant a site in Scottish social history. In another case one of the new County Buildings Trusts was able to rescue an entire terrace of early industrial housing from demolition — in the Golden Valley in Derbyshire (C 1980). Or a similar organisation in a historic country town such as Bradford-on-Avon would take on 'the town's largest unwanted building,' the dignified Queen Anne Silver Street House (C 1980), restore its facade and convert the interior to six flats and an office for itself.

Often a local civic society took a lead and was able to enlist the enthusiasm and financial backing of the local authorities, and through them of the Historic Buildings Council and other grant-giving bodies. This was how the restoration of the elegantly Grecian domed Waterworks in Perth (H 1975) and its conversion into a tourist information and exhibition centre got under way. Or, taking on board a less prestigious restoration, members got going and did the job by the sweat of their own brows. In Maidenhead a derelict Victorian footbridge (C 1980) was rebuilt, 'the only non-voluntary labour being the pile-driving and the placing of the main beams.' In Lewes the Old Tilting Ground lawn below the castle walls, previously surrounded by a shabby chain-link fence, is now walled in flint as though it always had been, entirely by voluntary labour and local fund-raising for the materials (C 1980). All over London local societies, often materialising *ad hoc* to meet a crisis, stepped in to defend a tiny corner from some highway or lighting nonsense, like the little tollhouse that slows up traffic

The Post Mill, Outwood Common, Surrey

Harthill Castle, in the Highlands of Scotland, restored by Mr and Mrs Stephen Remp

103

Berrington Hall, Leominster (before and after)

(Before)

The restored fronts and reorganised backs of a tenement in the Woodlands Area of Glasgow　*(After)*
Restoration in New Lanark　*Barnsbury Street, Islington, London*

Golden Valley, Derbyshire

Silver Street House, Bradford-on-Avon

Enfield, Gentleman's Row (before and after)

The Toll House, opposite the Spaniard's Inn, Hampstead, London (before and after)

Victorian Footbridge, Maidenhead, Berkshire

The Old Waterworks Building, Perth, Scotland

*Town Hall and Market,
Darlington*

*The New Weir, part of the flood
prevention scheme, River Avon,
Bath (opposite); Laying in the
power cable in Wasdale, Lake
District (below)*

opposite the Spaniards Inn in Hampstead (A 1967). It might be no more than the removal of a visual obstruction, as in Gentleman's Row, Enfield (C 1967). Often it was removing something, not building something, that did the trick, as with the National Trust's dramatic recovery of the courtyard elevation of Henry Holland's Berrington Hall near Leominster (A 1971). Or burying it. The laborious and costly burial of the electricity supply to Wasdale Head in the Lake District (A 1978) has saved the most awesome wild landscape in England.

It should not be supposed that all local authorities had to be badgered to act. Many took the lead themselves. The little town of Haddington in East Lothian, with a population of 6,000, has spent some £2 million since the early fifties on restoration, small-scale improvements and infill, instigated mainly by its Council, but including the remarkable rebuilding of the tower, choir and transepts of the large medieval church, which had been in ruins for centuries. Darlington, a good town often wrongly by-passed by tourists headed for Durham, rightly won a 1980 Award for the restoration and refurbishment of its Victorian Town Hall and Covered Market, signposted from afar by the handsome 'Flemish' clock tower, as well as a Commendation for the clean-up and conversion of the Georgian town houses close by. The colourful market scheme, done in perfect taste, without being 'tasteful,' is a smash-hit locally; and not far to the south is some new red brick housing of which the same can be said — an impeccable example of the current renaissance in housing design in Britain. Bath, forced to embark on a flood protection scheme on the Avon in the very heart of the city, made full use of their regular consultant and achieved a most satisfying weir (A 1972). 'Its steps, their great crescents cascading across the Avon, are views of foam in sparkling contrast to the quiet waters above them reflecting Pulteney

Custom House Quay, Glasgow, a before view (above) and as it is today (opposite)

The Piazza, Victoria Street, London (page 90)

Bridge. Passers-by stop to discover why others have stopped . . .' In some larger cities traffic schemes were initiated that enabled a great new central space to be paved for pedestrians. Portsmouth and Bolton (H 1975), with their almost identical late Victorian town halls, both did this with dramatic results. And Glasgow achieved the largest, best and most badly-needed piece of new urban landscape in Britain — the new Clyde Waterfront (H 1975). Starting in 1973 with Custom House Quay and the surroundings of the fine old Suspension Bridge, much helped by the Carlton House facelift on the opposite bank, this now stretches downstream for over a mile (now to be further extended) and brilliantly exploits its south aspect with all sorts of steps, ramps, terraces, seats and planting, in which fussiness and monotony are both avoided. Equally central but more accessible than Trafalgar Square, more sheltered than Liverpool's Pierhead, this is exactly what the grand, battered old city needed. The photographs of what it was like before are now historic documents. It would be good to know who designed it.

At the soft end of urban design, many made new parks or, to much better immediate effect, restored old ones. In Islington the oasis modestly called St.

The Trim Courses at Irvine Beech Park (left); and Livingston, Scotland (right)

The Rochdale Canal in the middle of Manchester (before and after)

Paul's Shrubbery (A 1973), re-landscaped in close consultation with the locals, has a sunk play-space that stops footballs from running under the feet of old people. Another (A 1972) highly original kids' amenity is the vast paddling pool in Manchester, created by the Council out of an old canal that runs, out of sight of the street dweller, for three miles through the heart of the city, with thirteen locks. Two Scottish New Towns have recently completed fun facilities for all ages. Irvine has reclaimed 150 acres of stinking industrial and chemical wasteland and made of it a modern version of Battersea Park on the windy shore of the Clyde estuary (A 1980); and Livingstone has built, on the wooded banks of the river Almond, a ruggedly designed 'Trim Course' or joggers' obstacle run of the kind you will find in Germany and Switzerland — a project with a progeny, one can be sure (A 1978).

But the true test of a local authority in these matters is its capacity to put it all together — new roads (if needed), new spaces, old spaces renewed, old buildings refurbished or converted, new ones cleverly and sympathetically inserted. Though several others run them close, I have chosen three cities as exemplary.

111

New meets old, Durham;

Durham

Two ancient cities deserve a section to themselves.

In Durham it was the University, intimately related to the cathedral and embedded in the old city since its foundation in 1832, which took the lead in the rehabilitation of the gloomy and shabby old lanes that led up to Palace Green. From the early sixties into the seventies old houses were cleaned and converted, and new students' lodgings knitted into the medieval fabric of the North Bailey and Owengate by architects intelligently chosen for their skill in this field. Grey brick Jevons House of Hatfield College (C 1968), the largest of these, smoothly fills in a long gap in the street side and at the back falls away with interesting changes of level to face an admirable neo-Georgian range by Vincent Harris. On the opposite edge of the peninsular escarpment, on a highly sensitive site between cathedral and castle, the Palace Green Library extension (A 1971) faced wholly (and more expensively) in rubble and ashlar and (for this architect) restrained in detail, slots neatly and with distinction into one of the great silhouettes of Europe. But the University's *chef d'oeuvre* is Dunelm House

Dunelm House the Wear gorge

Previous pages
*Dunelm House, New Elvet
elevation on the Durham skyline
(top); Department of Psychology
on the University Campus.*

*The Palace Green Library
extension*

(A 1968) the staff and student club which clings to the romantically wooded bank of the Wear gorge immediately opposite the towering Chapel of the Nine Altars. It belongs to the period of le Corbusier's greatest influence, to which the dramatisation of its circulation pattern and the irregular spacing of its window mullions bear witness. But it is pre-brutalist in its use of smooth natural concrete, which has weathered excellently to match the local stone, and in the elegance and delicacy of its planes of wall and roof. The latter, conspicuous from across the gorge, is clad in large concrete tiles, chevrons in section, which have also weathered happily, and the whole building, descending in great steps to match the flights of its wide tiled central corridor, is linked to and brilliantly complemented by the elegant and technically ingenious footbridge, perhaps its designer's masterpiece (A 1965), which joins it with the heart of the original university and the cathedral. Ivy and other indigenous planting have long since taken this delightful building into the company of its ancient and hallowed surroundings.

Out on the prosperous southern fringes of the little city is the University's post-war campus, rather American and diffuse among its dark groves and

sloping lawns with dramatic glimpses of the distant cathedral. J. S. Allen's Festival-style Applebey Building of 1951, now pleasantly dated, is still unexcelled in this area, though the beautifully landscaped but confusingly planned hexagons of dark brick Trevelyan College (A 1968) run it close — an early and confident use of what was to be the ruling style of a decade later. Higher up the slope, the Department of Psychology (C 1971), designed by the excellent architect who as a young associate had worked with J. S. Allen on the Applebey, has a rather industrial austerity in deliberate contrast with its pastoral situation and a stumpy tower.

Meanwhile the old city slept, not without some Town v Gown jealousy of the *nouveau-riche* cuckoo in its midst. It had in the later years of the war commissioned the locally-born planner Thomas Sharp to study its planning problems, and he had been the first to propose the inner ring road, bridging the Wear just north of Framwellgate Bridge, which thirty years later in a modified form was at last to take through traffic out of the peninsula and make possible the closing and paving of the steep shopping street (Silver Street), of the stony market-place with its famous Russian Horse, and of both the ancient bridges on

Milburngate Shopping Centre

to which the street emerges at each end. Coming to fruition with the local government changes of 1974 (A 1978) this was one of the most successful of such projects in Britain, both in the high quality of the materials used and in the design of the new road itself (C 1968) and of the inevitably conspicuous multi-storey car park in the Leazes Bowl. The project was finally rounded off by the co-ordinated clean-up (with 85 per cent Government support in 'Operation Eyesore') of the 28 properties in Silver Street which back on to the great view from across the river (H 1975) and by the commercial development of the Milburngate Centre (A 1978) on the west bank. This is, as it should be, a complex jumble of shops, restaurants, flats and parking, unified by dark brown brickwork and Welsh slate. It is a cosy, un-vulgar, small-town scheme, an enhancement even of Durham, which time and creepers can only improve.

The City's pedestrianisation and floorscape scheme (and opposite)

(Before)   *(After)*

Leeds

The fact that a city has collected an exceptional number of Awards and Commendations no doubt indicates a competitive and assiduous City Council, but could not have happened without the existence of planners and architects with a good eye for local character and townscape. Leeds was lucky in many ways. Its original core, alone among the great northern cities, has a firm Georgian rectangularity and quite an intimate Georgian scale; it lost few of its good buildings in the war (though it has since sacrificed some of its churches), and its industrial diversification and large white-collar population have kept it comparatively prosperous since. This rectangularity has helped, as with American cities, to give its taller buildings some relationship with one another, until one comes out on to the fringes beyond the Headrow, where they tend to stand about in the usual disorderly English way. Thus the shiny brown marble Lloyds Bank on Park Row (C 1979) does more for the central townscape, despite the clumsy 'tray' that carries its superstructure, than does the equally shiny brown Yorkshire Bank in Clay Pit Lane. The best things are nearly all in the original core. Along the Headrow, and opposite Sir Reginald Blomfield's prissy and already shabby range of 1930 shops, is the excellent red brick reconstruction and extension of St. Andrew's House; further along and almost opposite Broderick's great Town Hall is Victoria House, its handsome neo-classic stone frontage taken down and rebuilt with a sympathetic modern base and attic (both C 1979). West again, on the north side of the street, a more recent range of red brick buildings (Oxford House and the new Crown Courts) have been carefully composed to produce an immaculate foreground to the view of the

A carefully restored minaret on St Paul's House and the elevation to Park Square South (below)

121

Opposite page
One of the restored Shopping Arcades

Town Hall from that direction. All this is the mature work of architects with a sure eye for the totality of townscape. The opposite is true of the Westgate Swimming Pool complex (A 1969), an amusingly vulgar assemblage of late-sixties clichés, out on its own on a weedy and ill-maintained patch of grass. But the most spectacular example of the rehabilitation and conversion of a Victorian building is St. Paul's House (A 1979), the remarkable Saracenic terra-cotta warehouse that now, as a smart office building, faces north on to the rosebeds of the spruced-up and umbrageous St. Paul's Square. This is a triumph, and behind it the previously black and depressing St. Paul's Street is now bright and gay, its old warehouses interleaved with properly-scaled new office buildings in the fashionable red Accrington brick that looks better in Leeds than it ever did in its Lancashire home.

Commercial Leeds, without a single modern building of the first order, nevertheless teaches its sister cities one simple lesson, that soap and water, pedestrianisation and sensitive infill do more for day-to-day happiness than the major works of important architects. No need to emulate Chicago. The grid of foot-streets and colourful shopping arcades, common to 19th century cities all over the world, has in Leeds a snugness of scale that belies the city's size, and unharrassed by traffic one is continually surprised by nice details, ancient and modern (C 1972). Emerging on to City Square, flawed like so many Victorian spaces by the eccentric placing of its main building, but ingeniously re-paved (C 1963) to absorb the clash of alignments and to set off the heroic Black Prince on his black plinth, one finds that even the previously black G.P.O. has been cleaned and recently added to, this time in a matching tawny stone, and with the new sensibility one now finds in this city.

Lloyds Bank on Park Row (left);
St Andrews House

124

Norwich

Another ancient city, like Durham in the game from the start, achieved prodigies of small-scale improvement and deserves some paragraphs to itself. Post-war operations in Norwich have left the historic city a curate's egg. But if you shed your car and never go south of the Castle, you will have one of the happiest peregrinations in Europe, an object-lesson in the neo-picturesque, a colour-photographer's paradise, with every vista charmingly closed, every spruced-up miniscule courtyard worth peeping into and a dusky flint-faced church every few yards. It all started with Magdalen Street, scene of the very first Civic Trust 'face-lift' in 1959. The idea emerged when the Trust, seeking a means of demonstrating the potential released by co-operative effort, found this the project most acceptable to the City Engineer who was then in charge of planning. Misha Black's skilful chairmanship of the disparate participants did the rest. The choice of this street, with its narrow pavements and undivertable traffic, now seems an odd one, and of course it later had to be chopped in two by a flyover, but what remains at the near end looks all the better for some shabbiness and some repaints. Later, with the appointment of the enlightened A. A. Wood as City Planning Officer, Norwich achieved another first — the pedestrianisation of London Street (A 1969), still notable for its unaffected detail and excellent materials, from which other foot-streets were soon to ramify in all directions. Summer lunch hours see the whole maze abuzz with shoppers and tourists.

It was therefore a point of pride that Norwich should do something outstanding to mark European Architectural Heritage Year, 1975. 'Heritage over

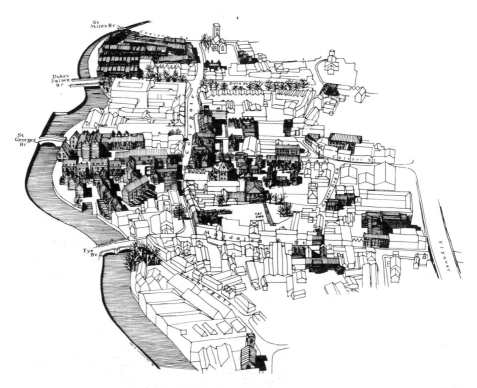

Drawing shows all the schemes
which formed the 'Heritage
Over the Wensum' project

125

Wensum,' as it was called (H 1975), was to be the rehabilitation of that whole ancient quarter north of the little river, once the preserve of successful merchants, radical non-conformist weavers, and all sorts of other skilled men, but later fallen into squalor and decay. Handsome churches and chapels, snug public houses, jettied gabled houses and red Georgian fronts still lined the narrow streets. The object was to restore and convert the old buildings, recover, replant and repave the open spaces and fill the gaps with appropriate new houses. 26 individual operations constituted the first phase, and it turned out an outstanding example of cheerful teamwork. Under the umbrella of the City Council's Conservation Panel were the Norwich Society, the Norwich over the Water Group, the Norwich Preservation Trust, the Norfolk Society of Architects, a specially constituted development company and a traders' association, which together co-ordinated the first-phase operations and planned future phases. To these were added a force of forty volunteers of all ages, many of them from youth organisations, using donated materials.

There are still jobs to be done, and always will be, but Norwich over the Water has now settled down, a casual mix of new and old, as was intended. Out-

Four schemes for the Wensum project — 22/24 Calvert Street, 2/4 Miles Alley, The Pope's Buildings, Fishergate Riverside Scheme

standing amid the new is Friar's Quay, a group of steep-roofed flats for single people along the water's edge in an ideally quiet yet central situation. This is a piece of perfect expertise by local architects internationally known for such work. One notes the subtle, just perceptible, variation in bricks and pointing, the romantic silhouette, the correct pitch of the pantiles into which even roof-lights fit quite happily, and the chimneys with their East Anglian hint of maltings. Other more recent infill is of variable quality — excellent in Calvert Street opposite the restored Pope's Buildings, horrific in Coslany Street. Norwich is of course an obstacle course for the urban knitter, but was nonetheless often ahead of other cities in being prepared to use awkward small sites for housing infill.

On the other side of the river, in the heart of the old town, wander down the aptly-named Pottergate and you will find the City Architect's modest and impeccable cottages (A 1972) slotted into a delightful group of buildings, but hard by a well-meant but overbearing red group of new flats called Ten Bell Court. This is traditional. If all Norwich were in the best taste it would be too good to be true, or too true to be good.

New Housing on Friars Quay

CHAPTER FOUR

Hindsights

These pages are unusual in bringing together a range of environmental endeavours not normally seen in juxtaposition — in books, that is; in real life these things jostle together, and it is their inter-relationship which so largely governs the character and 'feel' of a place — which makes this town pleasant to live and work in, that town a depressing non-event. Too often the different elements which make up our surroundings — the buildings, the roads, the landscaping, the underground services, the industrial facilities — are in fact dealt with in isolation, by a multitude of different agencies, mostly without much reference to one another. How refreshing to be reminded that they are only facets of a greater whole.

We have seen glimpses of how all our towns and cities might so easily be, if we only chose it so. There was nothing special about the places concerned, there were no secret resources to be drawn upon — people simply used their imagination, commissioned good architects and designers, and got on with it. Genius can look after itself. What we have a right to expect is a certain level of quality in our surroundings in all the day-to-day changes which are part of any living community, below which we *need* not accept what is offered. Manifestly there is no shortage of design talent in Britain; but to ensure that it is fully used, the pressure has all the time to be kept up on those who *commission* work, both official and unofficial. It is a matter of wanting quality enough to ensure we get it. We get, after all, the surroundings we deserve.

How buildings — and spaces, too, for that matter — 'work' for their users matters no less than how they look. So some readers may have been shocked by casual, man-in-the-street references to achievements which emerged, many of them, from a long process of research, experiment, small-hours inspiration and craftsmanship. For this, there were two reasons. First, the essence of what needed to be conveyed was quality-in-quantity. As Aldo van Eyck has put it: 'It is painfully true of architecture that it is not just good quality that counts, but a sufficient quantity of such quality. A good school in Amsterdam is of no use to a child in London (or vice versa)'. So a mention of 173 projects out of 2,780 seemed more appropriate than a fuller critique of half as many. And after all, the awards themselves were reconnoitred by busy architects motoring great distances, and were recommended on *environmental* grounds — because they enhanced, or even transformed, their surroundings. There seemed no point in

Redevelopment and Rehabilitation Central Area, Jedburgh

enlarging their own criteria.

Nevertheless, at the end of any long journey, it is worth trying to give some shape to a bundle of sensations, and this I will now attempt, grasping first the nettle of architecture itself. In its whole long history, there is no precedent for our contemporary emphasis on 'good manners.' The phrase was first used, I think, by Trystan Edwards as long ago as 1924, a voice crying in the wilderness of the 'By-Pass Variegated' age. The modernists saw themselves as the descendants of the great men of the past in looking askance at such servility. There was time-honoured authority for the view that so long as a new building was good of its kind, honestly of its own time, it would in due course take its proper place in the street-side story. Mousy attempts to 'fit in' risked a mediocre long-term effect, particularly if the neighbours one deferred to eventually disappeared themselves. And, of course, more positively, the modern movement in its early days was embattled against the forces of reaction. The first swallows of that spring, designers of the impeccably white flat-roofed houses, found themselves ordered by magistrates to choose between facing bricks and a tiled roof, and the beautiful Highpoint One had to fight off a violent onslaught from the Highgate Society. Modernism was never going to transform the quality of life if it knuckled under to that sort of obstruction.

In advising assessors that the awards are given 'for outstanding contributions to the environment' and that 'greater emphasis must therefore be given to this aspect of submissions than to the *purely architectural*,' the Trust knew it might be in for trouble. It would never do if the awards acquired a genteel image in the eyes of our brightest young architects. In fact it need not have worried. For one thing the assessors themselves were no fuddy-duddies, and a proportion of the awards duly went to glossy office towers, multi-storey flats, sophisticated university buildings and all the other showpieces of the sixties. They even, as we have seen, overdid it at times, with unpopular buildings like the Gorbals flats in Glasgow and the South Bank arts centre in London. And as time went on, in what some saw as a loss of nerve and others as a gain in sensibility, modernism itself moved from its purist phase into its mannerist one, in which pretty well anything was legitimate, and so side-stepped any conflict between 'architecture' and 'amenity.' It could now be claimed that the original Class 1 criterion ('New buildings . . . in the design of which respect has been paid to the character of neighbouring buildings, spaces and/or natural surroundings') applied to them all.

Then there is the question of photography. Photography is an existentialist skill that lends itself to surrealism better than it does to realism. On a normal soft grey day in Britain buildings photographed in black and white do not look themselves. So photographers wait for a bright contrasty one and find they do not look themselves either: shadows are over-dramatic and half the building is in the shade. As new buildings soften and improve with age they disimprove as subjects. Photography misleads as to scale and, hardest of all for the reader of this book, denies him the sense of space and the kinetic experience of walking around and through a building. This was the experience for which the awards were given — for environments, and not for art works intended to be admired in the Renaissance manner from controlled viewpoints. To enjoy them one really has to visit them. So the pictures in this book are for identification only, so that their subjects may take their place, as they deserve, among the life-enhancing sights of Britain.

Travelling among them, one is already conscious of their historical context. Until the mid-sixties mainline modernism characterised all the new buildings entered, and the environmental problem was seen traditionally as a marriage of old and new in which neither party was expected to sacrifice its individuality. Projects were on the whole large — mass housing, schools, universities, office blocks, factories — and on the whole new: in 1965 only 15 per cent of the awards went to restoration. Large organisations were still widely admired: in the London region in 1964 nine Awards and sixteen commendations went to the Architect's Department of the old London County Council, then the most prestigious public office in the world. But already in the early sixties there was disquiet about where the scale and urgency of our operations was leading us, and one saw the need for 'a new kind of architect' (whom I defined in 1959 as an 'environmentalist') who would possess 'the painstaking analysis, sense of growth, respect for the awkward fact and above all patience that are not often found in a designer. It is in some sense the differences between the surgeon with his spectacular drama and the GP whose background existence is only shown in the fact that people are well.' Otherwise, it would soon turn out that 'we prefer the slums.'

In the hinge year of the *événements,* 1968, the Civic Trust's report expressed the same anxieties. On the one hand there was a great improvement in motorway bridges design, but on the other there was nothing from the farmers, whose rejection of the craft tradition was now virtually total, and the recurrent plea for 'modesty and simplicity' was renewed. By the turn of the decade the Jekyll-and-Hyde phenomenon had become more pronounced. The Trust could describe 1970 as a turning-point in the campaign for conservation and write of 'the total awakening of the country throughout its regions,' and that 'more has been done in the past five or six years to renovate our towns, cities and countryside than over the previous century.' Yet in that same 1971 report, with vandalism rampant everywhere, it had to record 'the collapse of civic pride,' the 'brutality and havoc' created by developers and (once again) the excesses of 'architects who lack humility.' What was taking place was of course a classic case of schizophrenia only to be resolved by a change of consciousness, or by what Michael Middleton in an earlier chapter describes as the central aim of the Trust — 'to effect a fundamental shift of public opinion.' The shift in question was that we should all, producers and consumers alike, see new buildings not as isolated objects, whether good or bad, but as new threads in an ever-changing tapestry — a continuing heritage. Our obligation was always to this as a totality.

It followed that old and new were equivalent — of equal value. The Trust never took the extreme conservationist position that an old building restored and converted is always a happier solution and often a better investment than a new one. Such a view, common enough in the late seventies, would obviously be fatally damaging to architectural imagination. The fun was the mix — *vive la différence.* Nevertheless it could not be denied that there was a special pleasure to be got, both by doer and spectator, from the correct, ingenious and generous renewal and adaptation of old buildings, gardens and landscapes. There was for one ,thing the cheerful atmosphere of a national spring-clean: what was in hand was nothing less than the great clean-up after the Industrial Revolution. In a report of 1977 the Trust calculated that the crowded island had lost 250,000 acres of farmland to industrial waste in patches that varied in scale from a riverside garden (then a junkyard) in Norwich to the abandoned docks of London and Liverpool and on again to the devastated landscapes of Stoke, Swansea and the Black Country. It might be a century's reclamation work, but it had to be done, and with it went the removal of the monster's tentacles — the wirescape that disfigured every village and much of the landscape — and of its excreta — the soot and grime that encrusted all our best urban architecture. Again, the scale ran all the way from an isolated cottage in Gwynedd to whole villages like Harriston in Cumbria and Fordyce in Banff and so up to the spectacular unveiling of the Law Courts and the Albert Hall in London. Cosmetics only made sense if accompanied by the necessary surgery — cleaning out of gutters and downpipes, excision of rotten timbers and risky wiring, re-roofing, re-pointing, restoration of glazing bars, etc, etc. Craftsmen and workmen, it turned out, moved as merrily into this kind of familiar work as musicians into Mozart after the anxious note-by-note interpretation of a piece of architecture whose master concept had never been revealed to them.

What we now have is a transformation which, after ten years, we may have come to take for granted. If so, it is a good idea to cross the Channel. France, which had three times Britain's population when most of these old buildings were new and now has twice its wealth, does not choose to spend it this way. Outside the tourist's Paris and a few select *monuments historiques* the old parts of towns are as shabby as ever. Thousands of unwanted buildings stand about as they always did with peeled rendering exposing rough rubble and grey shutter slats hanging from rusted hinges. The pale oak framing of Normandy and the creamy stone of the Loire have been spared (one thankfully finds) our English cosmetics, and offer themselves still as subjects for a Cotman, a Turner or a Sickert. Nobody seems to bother about their date or their townscape value. This gives food for thought. You can take at least three views of a piece of woodland. To the naturalist a tree long past its prime is an indispensable habitat, to the artist an object of interest, to the forester a menace, liable to harbour diseases. Urban management offers similar alternatives, depending on whether one takes a social, aesthetic or commercial view. Moreover in England what we claim to be an aesthetic view often turns out to be more literary than visual. Melancholy thoughts occasioned by picturesque Victorian sketches of crumbling cottages and cheerful thoughts occasioned by the busy-bee activities of Suffolk commuters are equally literary: neither outcome is any more 'beautiful' than the other. So what are we to think of this whole unprecedented, and elsewhere unequalled, effort?

A visit to Magdalen Street, Norwich, 22 years after the famous first face-lift, may suggest some answers. The choice of this street for the treatment, no doubt for reasons of local politics, now seems eccentric. Since chopped in half by a subsequent flyover, it is nevertheless still infested with heavy lorry traffic, now a lot heavier; it is dangerous to cross the street to look at an elevation and anti-social to obstruct the narrow pavement trying to do so. One's first reaction is that what mattered in Norwich was to deal with the traffic problem rather than play about with colour schemes. And of course they did. Other foot-streets near the market-place, which escaped the 'treatment' but were cleared of traffic and just left to be themselves, work much better. Criticizing it at the time, one could see that that candy-pink, that lime-yellow, that Reckitt's blue, that fat Egyptian lettering, that white-painted timbering — off-shoots of the Festival of Britain and reflecting the colour-starved 1940s — would soon date. But 'it is no good worrying about this: we must do what our best people think good,' I wrote. Nobody would claim this now. Our best people have tumbled off their pedestals, and the thought of 'teams of architects,' each responsible for a length of street and for persuading its tradesmen into good taste, is now as comic as Dad's Army. Anyway the poor tradesmen have tumbled too — to takeovers sweetened by golden handshakes. Magdalen Street today, if you can stop to look at it, is like a gently *passé* spa, and all the better for the faded glory. What colour it was, or is, or will be, does not seem to matter.

But of course there was more to it than colour. Among the notables who strolled down the street on opening day, when it was cleared of traffic for an hour, was Gordon Russell, because *design* of street furniture, of signs, of fascias, of lighting, was very much at issue. The commercialisation of commercial streets, which has to mean their vulgarisation, was in that age of good causes something we had to contend with. Walt Whitman had taken a very different view. 'I do not doubt but the majesty and beauty of the world are latent in any iota of the world. I do not doubt there is far more in trivialities, insects, vulgar persons, dwarfs, weeds, rejected refuse, than I have supposed.'

Unless the myriad houses and workplaces of myriad men are to reflect this diversity, towns are going to be very odd places indeed, continually under treatment not because their inhabitants want them to be, but because in some stratosphere beyond their aspiration there has been a change of taste. This is one *reductio ad absurdum*. The other would be to throw design out of the window and let it all rip, as has indeed been seriously suggested in the recent reaction against planning. The Trust wisely kept clear of the continuing controversy about aesthetic control, bitterly resented by some architects and accepted as a social obligation by others. As far as the awards were concerned, the policy of picking highly regarded professional assessors and flanking them with representatives of local opinion was the only sensible course. But the question remains whether the whole apparatus has, as one would expect, tended to promote the safe and the decent and to discourage the eccentric and the outrageous — the kind of architecture which when it was done by Victorians, Edwardians and inter-war Art-Decorators we now delight to honour.

The answer is not as straightforward as one might expect. Magdalen Street has had an enormous, some would say monstrous, progeny. If its children were the 400 or 500 face-lifts that followed it in the sixties, its grandchildren of the seventies were the thousands upon thousands of do-it-yourself colour-allsorts in environments that varied in status from the High at Oxford to the back streets of Merseyside. All over Britain the decent terraces of our great-grandparents have been done over, in an ever more urgent search for personal identity, no two houses alike, pinky beige roughcast on old stone, fake Cotswold stonework on old brick, red cement tiles replacing slate, picture windows replacing casements. One cannot tell what Misha Black's teams of architects would have made of this, but I find it all intensely enjoyable, a visual embodiment of Whitman's aspirations. Safe and decent, though, it is not. Alongside this, in a remarkable juxtaposition, we have the middle-class world of the Conservation Areas, of Chipping Campden and Clare, of Haddington and Helmsley, where infinite pains are taken to 'get it right.' This is splendid too. Through its encouragement of individual initiative and care, however modest the individual intention and however prolonged the operation, the Trust had a hand in both outcomes. Indeed the claim for Magdalen Street is not that it imposed good taste, but that it invited the random inhabitants of an English street to use their eyes, for the first time to see it as a whole, to realise that improvement is within their power, and to get together to achieve it. By the time the awards were reinstituted in 1978 this realisation had such a momentum of its own that assessors could concentrate on the imaginative and the exceptional and need no longer commend projects just for happening at all. This is of course the best possible insurance against the charge of mediocrity.

Mediocrity there inevitably was, most obviously in the middle period between the moral collapse of evangelical modernism and the emergence of a new, un-dogmatic sensibility in the late seventies. You could hardly hand out some 140 awards and commendations on average a year without rewarding some of it. But it is surely not merely a liking for what we are doing now that enables one to claim that that stage is past. As early as 1973 the London assessors had virtua-lly stopped giving recognition to large projects, whether in the public or the private sector. That year's report noted with some pessimism that even in the inner boroughs a modest mews house was more likely to be commended that a major housing project. The pessimism was uncalled for: by 1978 local authority housing had shrunk itself to mews scale, and 'small is beautiful' assessors found plenty to admire.

The spread of awards across the country has for some years been pretty even. The Scottish lowlands have invariably scored well, and in England in the early years the North-West, with its own regional Civic Trust, had a head start, to be closely pursued by the North-East and East Anglia, but it was soon noticeable that it was not the tourist areas that necessarily did best: the Cotswolds for instance, stuck in a cautious 'vernacular' groove, had little of originality to offer. On the whole it was in the Northern industrial cities where courage was most needed that it was most forthcoming. In the same way, the early awards tended to be monopolised by a few expertly-staffed local authorities and a few architects of sensibility while the commercial herd galloped on regardless. More recently, the lessons having been learned, new regional names and reformed old ones have shown up, and for those in search of an architect in any part of the UK here is obviously the best possible directory.

So what is the verdict at this quarter-century milestone? Problems there have been both of definition and of administration. The scheme's very catholicity is a problem. 'Outstanding contributions to the environment' can be made by every conceivable kind of physical change. Not only architects, surveyors and engineers of all varieties but builders, farmers, foresters, landscapists, public utilities, extractive industries, manufacturers of paint, plastics, tiles, windows, caravans, agricultural buildings, bus shelters, lamp posts, TV aerials and every individual householder and landowner are involved. All new structures find themselves in some sort of relationship with what was there before, so no category excludes itself. Major works of architecture were obviously eligible yet it was important not to let them predominate. It is not surprising that all sorts of more narrowly defined and therefore easier to administer award schemes have followed since — too many in fact: it is particularly unfortunate that newspaper-sponsored Conservation Awards have moved into a vital sector of the Trust's coverage. Yet it is their catholicity that makes the Trust's annual reports on the awards so much more attractive than anybody else's. This is the last thing that should be sacrificed.

The educational achievement of the awards must have been substantial though it can never be quantified and is never completed. It cannot have been helped by the 1975 changes in local government, which have weakened the counties and boroughs that administered the scheme and promoted district councils that are seldom as well served. Planning officers still find sensible recommendations over-ruled by know-all committees wielding nothing better than power. The hysterical and ignorant assault on modern architecture in general that marked the journalism of the seventies still has its echoes, not least in 'educated' circles that should know better. So powerful is the pressure on Western intellectuals to be savagely critical of their own societies that congratulation has become a kind of royal or ministerial prerogative. The record in fact speaks for itself. Twenty-five years ago the clean-up of Britain had not begun. Flashy and often ill-considered new architecture rose out of a sea of muddle and squalor. The industrial wastelands were areas of nightmare, the ordinary run of Grade 2 historic buildings were in decay or mutilation, Conservation Areas did not exist and it was rare for house builders to save old trees or plant new ones. If one event signalled the turn of the tide it was the Civic Amenities Act of 1967, sponsored by the Trust's President. This seems to have given the civic societies, the historic buildings trusts, the Housing Associations and the army of *ad hoc* local groups the focus and impetus they needed. Local media became alert for news of local environmental crises and local government plucked up its courage to take the right side. To take three Award winners only, Newcastle at Byker, Norwich beyond the Wensum, and Milton Keynes almost all over, demonstrated that, if people feel that a genuine attempt is being made to meet their desires as well as their needs, there will emerge a huge fund of goodwill and collaboration — and there will be no vandalism. Conservation and improvement can go hand in hand — opposite sides of the same coin.

Of course the puzzle remains that in this as in other fields *video meliora proboque: deteriora sequor.* * The fact is that over the years the scheme has unearthed and publicised happy solutions in remarkable numbers, yet planning and housing agencies, developers, even the professions which should know better, still fail through lack or concern of lack of flexibility to make use of them. Architects find it easier to learn tricks of style than the patience and empathy from which in the end the most satisfying results emerge. And even where the initial choice was a good one, maintenance and modification are run by different people and let it down. This is where SPAN and Eric Lyons, with their residents' associations, got it right years ago, but have been too little imitated. Many local authorities have been equally remiss in this aspect of aftercare. So we have gained the experience, but not the habit, and the verdict can only be — 'a good start: keep it up!'

Finally we come to that 'fundamental shift' that was the ultimate objective. In the liberalisation, diversification, not to say permissiveness of contemporary architectural taste the Trust's role could not be dominant — changes of taste are more complicated than that — but has undoubtedly been influential. Assessors have unanimously given the new softer line a pat on the back. But the objective was wider than that. The real triumph of the Trust's awards

---

*I see and admire something better: I do something worse.

scheme is that it identifies itself (in the mixture of good luck and good judgment that brings most successes) with a national characteristic and a national mood — withdrawn, cautious, home-loving, past-loving, deeply attached to the symbols that represent security, yet at the same time, given half a chance, ingenious and exceptionally capable of voluntary co-operative work. For acting out attitudes like these in the environmental field, if you do it with a certain style, you receive a prize. It is a return to simple pieties, to the creed of our forefathers and to the moral responsibility of the individual. It is in other words not a renaissance but a reformation, and as such, one must suppose, more in our line.

Appendix

Guidance Notes for Assessors (abbreviated)

The Trust issues guidance notes for use by assessing teams. The more important points may be summarized as follows:

— The essential nature of the Trust's awards is that they are given specifically for outstanding contributions to the environment. Greater emphasis must therefore be given to this aspect of submissions than to the purely architectural.

— Any creative work which contributes to the quality and appearance of townscape or landscape is eligible.

— Schemes will not be considered eligible unless the surroundings forming part of the total design have been completed within the specified period. Every building may be said to be surrounded by a 'zone of influence' — an area which directly affects, and is affected by, the buildings concerned. It is the very nature of Civic Trust Awards that they must embrace the design and execution of such areas.

— Problems may arise in relation to large-scale developments which are programmed for construction in successive phases. No hard-and-fast rule can be laid down, but it is suggested that while a commendation may be felt appropriate for a phase of such a development, Awards should normally be given only when the scheme is fully completed.

— Cases have arisen where, after an Award has been announced, publicity has been given to alleged defects in a scheme's construction or interior planning. Assessors are asked to satisfy themselves as far as is practicable that schemes recommended for Award or commendation are unlikely to attract this kind of criticism. Assessors are also asked to inform themselves, to a reasonable degree, of the back history of redevelopment schemes — in particular the extent to which schemes may have involved the destruction of historic buildings and/or landscapes.

— Assessors are particularly asked to consider the design of buildings from the point of view of future maintenance and weathering of the exterior. Schemes which could lose their 'good looks' within a year or two cannot be considered for an Award.

— If a consultant is required to give guidance on landscaping, engineering or historical authenticity, this can be arranged by the Trust.

Picture Credits

Grateful acknowledgement is made to the following for permission to reproduce photographs. We would also like to acknowledge all applicants and photographers who have submitted photographs over the years and who are too numerous to mention.

J Allan Cash 105 (Spaniards Inn, both); Archangel 104; Architects Journal 72, 87, 93 (left); Arup Associates 46 (top), 92 (both); Ashby & Horner Ltd 59 (top); Berger Photographics 94 (right centre); Crispin Boyle (Clifford Calpin & Partners) 98; Brecht–Einzig Ltd 54 (bottom right), 58, 67, 79 (top), 88 (bottom), 96 (bottom left), 100 (bottom); Birmingham, City of 53; British Railways Board 101 (bottom); British Tourist Authority 28; Calderdale, Borough of 44 (bottom); Countryside Commission 41 (top); Department of the Environment, Edinburgh 20 (bottom), 30 (both); John Donat 84, 91 (top), 112, 113, 114 (top); Durham, City of 119; Lionel Esher 50 (top right), 66 (top); Dr W H Findlay 105 (bottom right); Frederick Gibberd & Partners 63 (top); Greater London Council 49 (top), 68, 69, 100 (top); H J Heinz & Co 94 (top); Hemmingways 120; Ironbridge Gorge Museum Trust 52; Batchaza Korab 88 (top); Land use Consultants 36 (top); London Press photos 61 (top right); Mann Brothers 80 (top right); National Trust for Scotland 46 (bottom); Newcastle, City of 64; Ove Arup & Partners 9; James Parr & Partners 73 (top); Phillips Cutler, Phillips Troy 73 (bottom); Kenneth Prater 59 (top); Redland Brick 59 (bottom); Shepherd Construction Limited, York 42; Henk Snoek 47, 50 (centre), 96 (bottom right), 99 (bottom); Stoke on Trent, City of 36; Tayler & Green 65 (right); Sir Percy Thomas Partnership 74 (bottom); Washington Development Corporation (back cover); University of York 74 (top).

Index

Nearly all environmental work calls for a range of contributions from multi-disciplinary teams and different agencies. This is fully recognized by the Trust when making its Awards and commendations. It is a matter of regret that demands on space make it impossible here to note more than the principal designers for each scheme.